Just Plain Funny

by

Charles R. Smith

RoseDog Books

PITTSBURGH, PENNSYLVANIA 15222

RoseDog Books
701 Smithfield Street
Pittsburgh, PA 15222
Visit our website at *www.rosedogbookstore.com*

ISBN: 978-1-4349-3089-7
eISBN: 978-1-4349-7157-9

Table of Contents

- Help One Another---1
- The Earring --2
- Northern Arizona---3
- The Tomato Garden--4
- Kids & Bad Words---5
- Dumbest Kid in the World…uhuh ----------------------------------6
- Power of Prayer --7
- Getting Older--8
- Little Boy Firefighter ---10
- Military Humor ---11
- Ralph & the IRS --12
- Employee Handbook---14
- "Titanic" & "My Life" --16
- Police Officer & The Lawyer---18
- 15 Police Comments--20
- Please Tell me this won't Happen to Me--------------------------22
- Things you'd love to say at work, but don't----------------------25
- As you go through life there are times when things strike you as funny such as ------------------------27
- Got to love Grandmas--28
- 19 Guidelines to maintain a healthy level of Insanity ------------29
- Dogs are Expensive --31
- Dogs are smart-Especially old Dogs--------------------------------32
- California --34

- Man's Thinking --36
- Baby Pictures ---38
- Boy's will be Boy's --40
- Senior Citizens ---41
- Dear Abby --42
- Car ---43
- Don't you wish you could just say…? ---------------------------44
- Equal Opportunity--46
- Well what did you expect? --------------------------------------47
- Men Remember ---48
- Men ---49
- Old Men --51
- Older People --52
- Kids Do Listen --53
- Some Really Dumb Stuff to Think About -----------------------54
- State Fair --56
- Lawyer --57
- The Blind Man--58
- They Walk Among Us---59
- When Heaven Calls ---61
- The Follower --62
- Wisconsin ---63
- The Work Place ---64
- Christmas Golf--67
- Great Truths --68
- For people 50 Years or Older & especially for the Youth --------70
- Actual Writings on Hospital Charts -----------------------------72
- Did you Ever Wonder Why? ------------------------------------74
- Da Vinci Code --76
- Top 35 Oxymorons ---77
- Good Baptist --79
- Cissy & George ---80
- The Best Headlines of 2003--------------------------------------81
- The Preachers Son--82
- Language Barrier ---83
- Ole's Answer --84
- Just Trivia & More Trivia --86

- Cowboy Story --88
- Children and the Church--90
- Flight Chatter ---92
- A Woman's Random Thoughts--95
- I Wanna Take it Back --96
- Navajo message for the moon ---98
- Happy Thanksgiving --99
- The American Soldier--100
- Fly a Kite---101
- Bubba's Psychiatrist --102
- Noah In The Year---103
- The Guinness Book ---105
- Just Take the Money ---106
- Bull---107
- BS---108
- Miracle of Toilet Paper--109
- How to make a Woman Happy vs.113
  How to make a Man Happy--110
- Actual Australian Court Docket 12659 – Case of the
  Pregnant Lady---112
- A view into the not so Distant Future – Or is it----------------------113
- Teaching Math ---115
- Thoughts to Ponder on a Rainy Day ------------------------------------117
- Man's Rules for Women ---119
- Mothers Advise to her Daughter ---------------------------------------121
- The Telephone ---122
- Women? --124
- No Child Left Behind-In Massachusetts --------------------------------125
- 12 Zingers for the Ladies ---126
- What are Seniors Worth Anyway?--128
- 18 sure Fire ways you can tell when it's going
  to be a Rotten day--129
- Two Old Men swapping thoughts for the day ----------------------------130
- A Man has Needs ---132
- Marriage---134
- Got to love this Judge ---136
- Chapstick?---137

- Famous People Say some of the Dumbest Things ---------------139
- By my side! ---141
- Who said Blonds are not smart? ----------------------------------142
- Scottish Tooth Extraction---144
- Morons? ---145
- Possible Headlines in the year 2029 ------------------------------147
- Smart Old Man ---149
- Technology & People ---150
- Psychology does work --152
- Embarrassing Medical Exams! -------------------------------------153
- Sometimes --155
- 25 Signs you have grown up --------------------------------------156
- Wife from Hell---158
- Bubba --159
- Woman who knows her place --------------------------------------160
- Things that make you say hmmmm--------------------------------161
- What is our problem? ---163
- What a Difference 30 years makes---------------------------------165
- What a Difference a Century makes-------------------------------167
- Law Enforcement Humor --169
- Then and Now --170
- Thanksgiving Divorce --173
- Skills Test---174
- Sobriety Test---175
- The Rules ---176
- Blonds, Blonds & More Blonds------------------------------------178

Introduction

Humor is something that I have always had in my life. It has helped me in my profession as a teacher and coach for 33 years. It is what I love about my family and I look forward to when we get a chance to get together, primarily at Thanksgiving, Christmas, and Easter. The connection and love is primarily there because of God, but it is enhanced because of the humor we enjoy.

I have found humor is important in one's everyday life. Life is not easy and can cripple us in so many ways. Physically it can hurt our immunine system, and it can raise our stress hormones. It can cause physical pain to increase. It can make you tense. Mentally it can take the joy and zest out of life. It can raise your anxiety and fear level. It can cause stress and play havoc with your moods. Socially life's hardships can destroy relationships, break down teamwork, cause conflicts and make you feel all alone.

One should always make time to laugh, have a good time, and smile, chuckle, and even go for a good old fashioned belly laugh. When we do this we feel good.

Humor is infectious. The sound of laughter is contagious. Laughter is strong medicine for your mind, emotions, and Physical wellbeing.

You should always try smiling daily, just like taking vitamins. You should always count your blessing and be happy for them. When you hear laughter, move towards it, embrace it. Spend time with fun, playful people. Play and laugh with your family. Learn to laugh at yourself. Pay attention to children, learn from them. They are the masters at play and laughter.

This book is my attempt to enhance your life with some humor and by doing so I hope that I do the following: Make you smile, chuckle, or laugh out loud, reduces your stress level and improves your overall health. Take a cup of coffee find a comfortable place and just sit back and read some Just Plain Funny Stories. Hope you smile. (☺)

HELP ONE ANOTHER

A couple is in bed sleeping when there's a rat-a-tat-tat on the door. The husband rolls over and looks at the clock, and its half past 3 in the morning. "I'm not getting out of bed at this time," he thinks, and rolls over. Then, a louder knock follows. So he drags himself out of bed, goes downstairs, opens the door, and there's a man standing there. It didn't take the homeowner long to realize the man was drunk.

"Hi there," slurs the stranger. "Can you give me a push?" "No, get lost. It's half past three and I was in bed," says the man as he slams the door. He goes back up to bed and tells his wife what happened. She says, "That wasn't very nice of you. Remember that night we broke down in the pouring rain on the way to pick the kids up from the baby-sitter and you had to knock on that man's house to get us started again? What would have happened if he'd told us to get lost?"

"But the guy was drunk," says the husband. "It doesn't matter," says the wife." He needs our help and it would be the Christian thing to help him." So the husband gets out of bed again, gets dressed, and goes downstairs. He opens the door, and not being able to see the stranger anywhere, He shouts, "Hey, do you still want a push?" And he hears a voice cry out, "Yeah, please." So, still being unable to see the stranger he shouts, "Where are you?" The drunk replies. "Over here, on the swing." ☺

THE EARRING:

A man is at work one day when he notices that his co-worker is wearing an earring. This man knows his co-worker to be a normally conservative fellow, and is curious about his sudden change in "fashion sense." The man walks up to him and says, "I didn't know you were into earrings." "Don't make it such a big deal, it's only an earring." He replies sheepishly. His friend falls silent for a few minutes, but then his curiosity prods him to say, "So, how long have you been wearing one?" "Ever since my wife found it in my truck." (☺)

NORTHERN ARIZONA

A man is driving toward home in Northern Arizona when he sees a Navajo man hitchhiking. Because the trip had been long and quiet, he stops the car and the Navajo man climbs in. During their small talk, the Navajo man glances surreptitiously at a brown bag on the front seat between them. "If you're wondering what's in the bag," offers the man, "it's a bottle of wine. I got it for my wife" The Navajo man is silent for a while, nods several times and says, "Good trade." ☺

THE TOMATO GARDEN

An old man lived alone in the country. He wanted to dig his tomato garden, but it was much too difficult for him, as the ground was very hard. His only son, Vincent, who used to help him, was in prison. The old man wrote a letter to his son and described his predicament:

Dear Vincent,

I am feeling pretty bad because it looks like I won't be able to plant my tomato garden this year. I'm just getting too old to be digging up a garden plot. If you were here, my troubles would be over. I know you would dig the plot for me.
Love, Dad

A few days later, he received a letter from his son:

Dear Dad:

Not for nothing, but don't dig up that garden. That's where I buried the BODIES.
Love, Vinnie

At 4:00 the next morning, FBI agents and local police arrived and dug up the entire area, but found no trace of bodies. They apologized to the old man and left.

The next day, the old man received another letter from his son:

Dear Dad:

Go ahead and plant the tomatoes now. That's the best I could do under the circumstances.
Love, Vinnie

KIDS & BAD WORDS

A 6 year old and a 4 year old are upstairs in their bedroom; "You know what?" says the 6 year old. "I think it's about time we started cussing." The 4 year old nods his head in approval. The 6 year old continues. "When we go downstairs for breakfast, I'm gonna say something with hell and you say something with 'ass." The 4 year old agrees with enthusiasm.

When their mother walks into the kitchen and asks the 6 year old what he wants for breakfast, he replies, "Aw, hell, Mom, I guess I'll have some Cheerios." WHACK! He flies out of his chair, tumbles across the kitchen floor, gets up, and runs upstairs crying his eyes out, with his mother in hot pursuit, slapping his rear with every step. His mom locks him in his room and shouts, "You can just stay there until I let you out!"

She then comes back downstairs, looks at the 4 year old and asks with a stern voice, "And what do YOU want for breakfast, young man?" "I don't know," he blubbers, "But you can bet your ass it won't be Cheerios." ☺

DUMBEST KID IN THE WORLD...UHUH

A young boy enters a barber shop and the barber whispers to his customer, "This is the dumbest kid in the world. Watch while I prove it to you." The barber puts a dollar bill in one hand and two quarters in the other, then calls the boy over and asks, "Which do you want, son"? The boy takes the quarters and leaves. "What did I tell you"? said the barber. "That kid never learns!"

Later, when the customer leaves, he sees the same young boy coming out of the ice cream store. "Hey, son! May I ask you a question? Why did you take the quarters instead of the dollar bill"? The boy licked his cone and replied, "Because the day I take the dollar, the game's over."☺

POWER OF PRAYER

A blonde was driving down the street in a sweat because she had an important meeting and couldn't find a parking place. Looking up toward heaven, she said, "Lord, take pity on me. If you find me a parking place I will go to Mass every Sunday for the rest of my life and give up sex and tequila." Miraculously, a parking place appeared. She looked up again and said, "Never mind. I found one."

GETTING OLDER ☹

The Four Stages of Life:
1. You believe in Santa Claus.
2. You don't believe in Santa Claus.
3. You are Santa Claus.
4. You look like Santa Claus.

SUCCESS:
1. At age 4 success is - not peeing in your pants.
2. At age 12 success is - having friends.
3. At age 16 success is - having a driver's license.
4. At age 35 success is - having money.
5. At age 50 success is - having money.
6. At age 70 success is - having a driver's license.
7. At age 75 success is - having friends.
8. At age 80 success is - not peeing in your pants.

SIGNS OF MENOPAUSE:
1. You sell your home heating system at a yard sale.
2. You have to write post-it notes with your kids' name on them.
3. You change your underwear after you sneeze.

OLD IS WHEN:
1. Going bra-less pulls all the wrinkles out of your face.
2. You don't care where your spouse goes, just as long as you don't have to go along.
3. Getting a little action means I don't need fiber today.

4. Getting lucky means you find your car in the parking lot.
5. An all-nighter means not getting up to pee!

THINGS THAT OLD PEOPLE SIT AND THINK ABOUT:

- Wouldn't it be nice if whenever we messed up our life we could simply pres 'Ctr Alt Delete' and start all over?
- Just remember, if the world didn't suck, we'd all fall off.
- If raising children was going to be easy, it never would have started with something called labor!
- Brain cells come and brain cells go, but fat cells live forever.
- A good friend is like a good bra. Hard to find, Supportive, Comfortable, and Always close to your Heart.
- I used to eat a lot of natural foods until I learned that most people die of natural causes.
- The easiest way to find something lost around the house is to buy a replacement.
- Never take life seriously. Nobody gets out alive anyway.
- In the 60's people took acid to make the world weird. Now the world is weird and people take Prozac to make it normal.
- How is it one careless match can start a forest fire, but it takes a whole box to start a campfire?
- Who was the first person to look at a cow and say, "I think I'll squeeze these dangly things here and drink whatever comes out?"
- Who was the first person to say, "See that chicken there? I'm gonna eat the next thing that comes outta its Butt.
- If Jimmy cracks corn and no one cares, why is there a song about him?
- Do illiterate people get the full effect of alphabet Soup?

LITTLE BOY FIREFIGHTER

A firefighter is working on the fire engine outside the station when he notices a little boy next door in a little red wagon with little ladders hung of the sides and a garden hose tightly coiled in the middle. The boy is wearing a fire fighter's helmet. The wagon is being pulled by his dog and his cat. The fire fighter walked over to take a closer look. "That sure is a nice fire truck," the firefighter says with admiration. "Thanks" the boy says.

The firefighter looks a little closer and notices the boy has tied the wagon to his dog's collar and to the cat's testicles. "Little partner", the firefighter says, "I don't want to tell you how to run your rig, but if you were to tie that rope around the cat's collar too, I think you could go faster." The little boy replies thoughtfully, "You're probably right sir, but then I wouldn't have a siren."

MILITARY HUMOR

Fifty –one years ago, Herman James, a North Carolina mountain man, was drafted by the Army. On his first day in basic training, the Army issued him a comb. That afternoon the Army barber sheared off all his hair. On his second day, the Army issued Herman a toothbrush. That afternoon the Army dentist yanked seven of his teeth. On the third day, the Army issued him a jock strap. The Army has been looking for Herman for 51 years.

RALPH & THE IRS

The IRS decides to audit Ralph, and summons him to the IRS office. The IRS auditor is not surprised when Ralph shows up with his attorney. The auditor says, "Well, sir, you have an extravagant lifestyle and no full-time employment, which you explain by saying that you win money gambling. I'm not sure the IRS finds that believable."

"I'm a great gambler, and I can prove it," says Ralph. "How about a demonstration?" The auditor thinks for a moment and said, "Okay. Go ahead." Ralph says, "I'll bet you a thousand dollars that I can bite my own eye." The auditor thinks a moment and says, "No way! It's a bet." Ralph removes his glass eye and bites it. The auditor's jaw drops. Ralph says, "Now, I'll bet you two thousand dollars that I can bite my other eye." The auditor can tell Ralph isn't blind, so he takes the bet. Ralph removes his dentures and bites his good eye. The stunned auditor now realizes he has wagered and lost three grand, with Ralph's attorney as a witness. He starts to get nervous. "Want to go double or nothing?" Ralph asks. "I'll bet you six thousand dollars that I can stand on one side of your desk and pee into that wastebasket on the other side, and never get a drop anywhere in between."

The auditor, twice burned, is cautious now, but he looks carefully and decides there's no way this guy can manage that stunt, so he agrees again. Ralph stands besides the desk and unzips his pants, but although he strains mightily, he can't make the stream reach the wastebasket on the other side, so he pretty much urinates all over the desk.

The auditor leaps with joy, realizing that he has just turned a major loss into a huge win. But Ralph's attorney moans and puts his head in his hands. "Are you okay?" the auditor asks. "Not really," says the attorney. "This morning, when Ralph told me he'd been summoned for an audit, he bet me twenty thousand dollars that he could come in here and urinate all over an IRS official's desk and that you'd be happy about it."☺

EMPLOYEE HANDBOOK

1. Dress Code ☺

    You are advised to come to work dressed according to your salary. If we see you wearing Prada shoes and carrying a Gucci bag, we will assume you are doing well financially and therefore do not need a raise. If you dress poorly, you need to learn to manage your money better, so that you may buy nicer clothes, and therefore you do not need a raise. If you dress just right, you are right where you need to be and therefore you do not need a raise.

2. Sick Days ☺

    We will no longer accept a doctor's statement as proof of sickness. If you are able to go to the doctor; you are able to come to work.

3. Personal Days

    Each employee will receive 104 personal days a year. (They're called Saturdays & Sundays.)

4. Bereavement Leave ☺

    This is no excuse for missing work. There is nothing you can do for dead friends, relatives or co-workers. Every effort should be made to have non-employees attend the funeral arrangements. In rare cases where employee involvement is necessary; the funeral should be scheduled in the late afternoon. We will be glad to allow you to work through your lunch hour and subsequently leave one hour early.

5. Bathroom Breaks ☺

    Entirely too much time is being spent on the toilet. There is now a strict three-minute time limit in the stalls. At the end of three minutes, an alarm will sound, the toilet paper roll will retract, the stall door will open, and a picture will be taken. After your second offense, your picture will be posted on the company bulletin board under the "Chronic Offenders" category. Anyone caught smiling in the picture will be sectioned under the company's mental health policy.

6. Lunch Break ☺

    Skinny people get 30 minutes for lunch, as they need to eat more, so that they can look healthy. Normal size people get 15 minutes for lunch to get a balanced meal to maintain their average figure. Chubby people get 5 minutes for lunch, because that's all the time need to drink a slim-Fast.

☺☺☺

Thank you for your loyalty to our company. We are here to provide a positive employment experience. Therefore, all questions, comments, concerns, complaints, frustrations, irritations, aggravations, insinuations, allegations, accusations, contemplation's, consternation and input should be directed elsewhere.

The Management ☺

"TITANIC" & "MY LIFE"

STUDENTS WERE ASSIGNED TO READ two BOOKS, "TITANIC" & "MY LIFE" BY BILL CLINTON. One smart student turned in the following book report, with the proposition that they were nearly identical stories! His cool professor gave him an A+ & a smile for this report:

Titanic : $ 29.99
Clinton : $ 29.99
Titanic : Over 3 hours to read
Clinton : Over 3 hours to read
Titanic : The story of jack and Rose, their forbidden love, and subsequent Catastrophe.
Clinton : The story of Bill and Monica, their forbidden love, and subsequent Catastrophe.
Titanic : Jack is a starving artist.
Clinton : Bill is a BS artist.
Titanic : In one scene, Jack enjoys a good cigar.
Clinton : Ditto for Bill.
Titanic : During fun, Rose's dress gets ruined.
Clinton : Ditto for Monica.
Titanic : Jack teaches Rose to spit.
Clinton : Let's not go there.
Titanic : Rose gets to keep her jewelry.
Clinton : Monica's forced to return her gifts.
Titanic : Rose remembers Jack for the rest of her life.
Clinton : Clinton doesn't remember Jack.

Titanic : Rose goes down on a vessel full of seamen.
Clinton : Monica…ooh, let's not go there, either
Titanic : Jack surrenders to an icy death.
Clinton : Bill goes home to Hilary…basically the same thing. ☺

POLICE OFFICER & THE LAWYER

If you ever testify in court, you might wish you could have been as sharp as this policeman. He was being cross-examined by a defense attorney during a felony trial. The layer was trying to undermine the policeman's credibility...

Q : "Officer – did you see my client fleeing the scene?"
A : "No sir. But I subsequently observed a person matching the description of the offender, running several blocks away."
Q : "Officer – who provided this description?"
A : "The officer who responded to the scene."
Q : "A fellow officer provided the description of this so-called offender. Do you trust your fellow officers?"
A : "Yes, sir. With my life."
Q : "With your life? Let me ask you this then officer. Do you have a room where you change your clothes in preparation for you daily duties?"
A : "Yes sir, we do!"
Q : "And do you have a locker in the room?"
A : "Yes sir, I do."
Q : "And do you have a lock on your locker?"
A : "Yes sir."
Q : "Now why is it, officer, if you trust your fellow officers with your life, you find it necessary to lock your locker in a room you share with these same officers?"

A : "You see, sir – we share the building with the court complex, and sometimes lawyers have been known to walk through that room."

The courtroom erupted in laughter, and a prompt recess was called. The officer on the stand won the case. ☺

15 POLICE COMMENTS

The following 15 police comments were taken from actual Dallas Police car videos and distributed by Monica Smith, Director DPDE, Public Relations Officer:

1. "Relax; the handcuffs are tight because they're new. They'll stretch out after you wear them awhile."
2. "Take you hands off the car, and I'll make your birth certificate a worthless document."
3. "If you run, you'll only go to jail tired."
4. "So you don't know how fast you were going. I guess that means I can write anything I want on the ticket, huh?"
5. "Can you run faster than 1200 feet per second?"
6. "Yes sir, by all means you can talk to the shift supervisor if you think it will help. Oh, did I mention that I am the shift supervisor?"
7. "Warning? You want a warning? O.K., I'm warning you that when you run that stop sign again, I'll give you another ticket."
8. "The answer to this last question will determine whether you are drunk or not. Was Mickey Mouse a cat or a dog?"
9. "Fair? You want me to be fair? Listen pal, fair is a place where you go to ride on rides, eat cotton candy, and step in horsey doo!"
10. "Yeah, we have a quota. Two more tickets and my wife gets a toaster oven."
11. "No sir, we don't have quotas anymore. We used to have quotas, but now we're allowed to write as many tickets as we want."
12. "Just how big were those two beers?"

13. "In God we trust, all others we run through the records department."

14. "I'm glad to hear the Chief of Police is a good personal friend of yours. At least you know someone who can post your bail."

15. "Excuse me ma'am? You didn't think we give pretty women tickets? Well, you are right, we don't. Now, sign here. ☺

PLEASE TELL ME THIS WON'T HAPPEN TO ME

1. 911! An elderly Floridian called 911 on her cell phone to report that her car has been broken into. She is hysterical as she explains her situation to the dispatcher; "They've stolen the stereo, the steering wheel, the brake pedal and even the accelerator!" she cried. The dispatcher said, "Stay calm. An officer is on the way." A few minutes later, the officer radios in. "Disregard." He says. "She got in the back-seat by mistake.

2. FAMILY – Three sisters age 92, 94 and 96 live in a house together. One night the 96 year old draws a bath. She puts her foot in and pauses. She yells to the other sisters, "Was I getting in or out of the bath?" The 94 year old yells back, "I don't know. I'll come up and see." She starts up the stairs and pauses "Was I going up the stairs or down?" The 92 year old is sitting at the kitchen table having tea listening to her sisters. She shakes her head and says, "I sure hope I never get that forgetful, knock on wood." She then yells, "I'll come up and help both of you as soon as I see who's at the door."

3. "I CAN HEAR JUST FINE!" Three retirees, each with a hearing loss, were playing golf one fine March day. One remarked to the other, "Windy, isn't it?" "No," the second man replied, "it's Thursday." And the third man chimed in, "So am I. Let's have a beer."

4. NURSING HOME! A little old lady was running up and down the halls in a nursing home. As she walked, she would flip up the hem of her nightgown and say "Supersex." She walked up to an elderly man in a wheelchair. Flipping her gown at him, she said, "Supersex." He sat silently for a moment or two and finally answered, "I'll take the soup."

5. DOWN AT THE FRETIREMENT CENTER! 80 – YEAR OLD Bessie bursts into the rec room at the retirement home. She holds her clenched fist in the air and announces, "Anyone who can guess what's in my hand can have sex with me tonight!" An elderly gentleman in the rear shouts out, "An elephant?" Bessie thinks a minute and says, "Close enough."

6. OLD FRIENDS! Two elderly ladies had been friends for many decades. Over the years, they had shared all kinds of activities and adventures. Lately, their activities had been limited to meeting a few times a week to play cards. One day, they were playing cards when one looked at the other and said, "Now don't get mad at me... I know we've been friends for a long time... but I just can't think of your name! I've thought and thought, but I can't remember it. Please tell me what your name is." Her friend glared at her. For at least three minutes she just stared and glared at her. Finally she said, "how soon do you need to know?'

7. SENIOR DRIVING! As a senior citizen was driving down the freeway, his car phone rang. Answering, he heard his wife's voice urgently warning him, "Jack, I just heard on the news that there's a car going the wrong way on interstate 77. Please be careful!" "Heck," said Jack, "It's not just one car. It's hundreds of them!"

8. DRIVING! Two elderly women were out driving in a large car – both could barely see over the dashboard. As they were cruising along, they came to an intersection. The stoplight was red, but they just went on through. The woman in the passenger seat thought to herself "I must be losing it. I could have sworn we just went through a red light." After a few more minutes, they came to another intersection and the light was red again. Again, they went right through. The woman in the passenger seat was almost sure that the light had been red but was really concerned that she was losing it. She was getting nervous. At the next intersection, sure

enough, the light was red and they went on through. So, she turned to the other woman and said, "Mildred, did you know that we just ran through three red lights in a row? You could have killed us both!" Mildred turned to her and said, "Oh, %!@#!, am I driving?"

TELL ME THIS WON'T HAPPEN TO ME!!!

THINGS YOU'D LOVE TO SAY AT WORK, BUT DON'T...

* I can see your point, but I still think you're full of #@&%@.
* How about never? Is never good for you?
* I see you've set aside this special time to humiliate yourself in public.
* I'll try being nicer if you'll try being smarter.
* I'm out of my mind, but feel free to leave a message.
* I don't work here, I'm a consultant.
* It sounds like English, but I don't understand a word you're saying.
* Ahhh...I see the screw-up fairy has visited again.
* I like you. You remind me of me when I was young and stupid.
* You are validating my inherent mistrust of strangers.
* I have plenty of talent and vision. I just don't give a damn.
* I'm already visualizing the duct tape over your mouth.
* Thank you. We're all refreshed and challenged by your unique point of view.
* The fact that no one understands you doesn't mean you are an artist.
* Any connection between your reality and mine is purely coincidental.
* What am I? Fly paper for freaks?
* I'm not being rude. You're just insignificant.
* Do I look like a frigging people person?
* This isn't an office. It's Hell with fluorescent lighting.
* Sarcasm is just one more service we offer.
* If I throw a stick, will you leave?

* Errors have been made. Others will be blamed.
* A cubicle is just a padded cell without a door.
* Too many freaks, not enough circuses.
* Chaos, panic and disorder...My work here is done.
* How do I set a laser printer to stun?
* I thought I wanted a career; turns out I just wanted pay checks.

AS YOU GO THROUGH LIFE THERE ARE TIMES WHEN THINGS STRIKE YOU AS FUNNY SUCH AS:

1. The difference between the Pope and your boss... the pope only expects you to kiss his ring.
2. My mind works like lightening. One brilliant flash and it is gone.
3. The only time the world beats a path to your door is if you're in the bathroom.
4. I hate sex in the movies. Tried it once. The seat folded up, the drink spilled and that ice, well, it really chilled the mood.
5. It used to be only death and taxes were inevitable. Now, of course, there's shipping and handling, too.
6. A husband is someone who, after taking the trash out, gives the impression that he just cleaned the whole house.
7. A blonde said, "I was worried that my mechanic might try to rip me off. I was relieved when he told me all I needed was turn signal fluid."

GOT TO LOVE GRANDMAS

Here's a quote from a government employee who witnessed a recent interaction between an elderly woman and an antiwar protestor in a Metro station in DC:

There were protestors on the train platform handing out pamphlets on the evils of America. I politely declined to take one. An elderly woman was behind me getting off the escalator and a young (Twenty) female protestor offered her a pamphlet, which she politely declined. The young protestor put her hand on the old woman's shoulder as a gesture of friendship and in a very soft voice said, "Lady, don't you care about the children of Iraq?" The old woman looked up at her and said, "Honey, my father died in France during World War II, I lost my husband in Korea, and a son in Vietnam. All three died so you could have the right to stand here and bad mouth our country. If you touch me again, I'll stick this umbrella up your ass and open it! ☺

19 GUIDELINES TO MAINTAIN A HEALTHY LEVEL OF INSANITY (☺) (☹)

- At lunch time, sit in your parked car with sunglasses on and point a hair dryer at passing cars. See if they slow down.

- Page yourself over the intercom. Don't disguise you voice.

- Every time someone asks you to do something, ask if they want fries with that.

- Put you garbage can on your desk and label it "IN"... Put decalf in the coffee maker for 3 weeks. Once everyone has gotten over their caffeine addiction, switch to espresso.

- Finish all your sentences with "In accordance with the prophecy."

- Don't use any punctuation.

- As often as possible, skip rather than walk.

- Order Diet water whenever you go out to eat – with a serious face.

- Specify that your drive-through order is, "to go!"

- Sing along at the opera.

- Put mosquito netting around your work area and play tropical sounds all day at work.

- Go to a poetry recital and ask why the poems don't rhyme.

- Five days in advance, tell your friends you can't attend their party because you're not in the mood.

- Have your coworkers address you by your wrestling name, Skull Crusher.

- When the money comes out the ATM, scream "I won! I won!"

- When leaving the zoo, start running towards the parking lot yelling, "Run for your lives, they're loose!"

- Tell your children over dinner "due to the economy, we are going to have to let one of you go."

- And the final way to keep a healthy level of insanity. Always blame the dog when you pass gas. Even if you do not own a dog. ☺

DOGS ARE EXPENSIVE

(Got to love them)

A visit to the Veterinarian:

A lady rushes into a veterinarian and screams, "I found my dog unconscious and I can't wake him, do something please!"

The vet goes into the other room, and comes back with a little cat. The cat jumps up on the table and starts sniffing the dog from head to toe. It sniffs and sniffs up and down the dog, then all of a sudden just stops and jumps off the table and leaves. "Well, that confirms it," the vet says, "Your dog is dead."

The lady is very upset but finally settles down. "Okay, I guess you're right. How much do I owe you?" The vet says, "That will be $340."

The lady has a fit and asks, "Why is it so much? You didn't do anything for the dog."

"Well", the vet replied, "its $40 for the office visit and $300 for the CAT SCAN!" ☺

DOGS ARE SMART – ESPECIALLY OLD DOGS ☺

A wealthy old lady decides to go on a photo safari in Africa, taking her faithful aged poodle named Cuddles, along for the company.

One day the poodle starts chasing butterflies and before long, Cuddles discovers that he's lost. Wandering about, he notices a leopard heading rapidly in his direction with the intentions of having lunch.

The old poodle thinks, "Oh, oh! I'm in deep doo-doo now!" Noticing some bones on the ground close by, he immediately settles down to chew on the bones with his back to the approaching cat. Just as the leopard is about to leap the old poodle exclaims loudly, "Boy, that was one delicious leopard! I wonder if there are any more around here."

Hearing this, the young leopard halts his attack in mid-strike, a look of terror comes over him and he slinks away into the trees.

"Whew!' says the leopard, "That was close! That old poodle nearly had me!" Meanwhile, a monkey who had been watching the whole scene from a nearby tree, figures he can put this knowledge to good use and trade it for protection from the leopard.

So off he goes, but the old poodle sees him heading after the leopard with great speed, and figures that something must be up.

The monkey soon catches up with the leopard, spills the beans and strikes a deal for himself with the leopard.

The young leopard is furious at being made a fool of and says, "Here, monkey, hop on my back and see what's going to happen to that conniving canine!"

Now, the old poodle sees the leopard coming with the monkey on his back and thinks, "What am I going to do now?", but instead of running, the dog sits down with his back to his attackers, pretending he hasn't seen them yet, and just when they get close enough to hear, the old poodle says: "Where's that damn monkey? I sent him off an hour ago to bring me another leopard!"

Moral of this story ☺

Don't mess with old dogs… age and treachery will always overcome youth and skill! BS and brilliance only come with age and experience!

CALIFORNIA (☺)

Not to be outdone by all the redneck, hillbilly, & Texan jokes...
You know you're in California when...

1. Your coworker has 8 body piercings and none are visible.
2. You make over $300,000 and still can't afford a house.
3. You take a bus and are shocked at two people carrying on a conversation In English.
4. Your child's 3rd grade teacher has purple hair, a nose ring, and is named Breeze.
5. You can't remember...is pot illegal?
6. You've been to a baby shower that has two mothers and a sperm donor.
7. You have a very strong opinion about where your coffee beans are grown, and you can taste the difference between Sumatran & Ethiopian.
8. You know which restaurant serves the freshest arugula.
9. You can't remember...is pot illegal?
10. A really great parking space can totally move you to tears.
11. A low speed police pursuit will interrupt any TV broadcast.
12. Gas cost $1.00 per gallon more than anywhere else in the U.S.
13. A man gets on the bus in full leather regalia and crotch-less chaps. You don't even notice.
14. Unlike back home, the guy at 8:30 am at Starbucks wearing the baseball cap and sunglasses who looks like George Clooney really is George Clooney.

15. Your car insurance cost as much as your house payment.
16. Your hairdresser is straight, your plumber is gay, the woman who delivers your mail is into S&M, and your Mary Kay rep is a guy in drag.
17. You can't remember...is pot illegal?
18. It's barely sprinkling rain and there's a report on every news station: STORM WATCH 2011.
19. You have to leave the big company meeting early because Billy Blanks himself is teaching the 4:00 Tae Bo class.
20. You pass an elementary school playground and the children are all busy with their cells or pagers.
21. It's barely sprinkling rain outside, so you leave for work an hour early to avoid all the weather-related accidents.
22. Hey!!! Is Pot illegal?
23. Both you and your dog have therapists.
24. The Terminator was your governor. Now we have Jerry Brown (☺)

MAN'S THINKING

- How many men does it take to open a beer? None. It should be opened when she brings it.
- Why is a Laundromat a really bad place to pick up a woman? Because a woman who can't even afford a washing machine will probably never be able to support you.
- Why do women have smaller feet than men? It's one of those "evolutionary things" that allows them to stand closer to the kitchen sink.
- How do you know when a woman is about to say something smart? When she starts a sentence with "A man once told me…"
- How do you fix a woman's watch? You don't. There is a clock on the oven.
- Why do men fart more than women? Because women can't shut up long enough to build up the required pressure.
- If your dog is barking at the back door and your wife is yelling at the front door, who do you let in first? The dog, of course. He'll shut up once you let him in.
- What's worse than a Male Chauvinist Pig? A woman who won't do what she's told.
- I married a Miss Right. I just didn't know her first name was Always.
- Scientist has discovered a food that diminishes a woman's sex drive by 90%. It's called a Wedding Cake.
- Why do men die before their wives? They want to.

- Women will never be equal to men until they can walk down the street with a bald head and a beer gut, and still think they are sexy.
- In the beginning, God created the earth and rested. Then God created Man and rested. Then God created Woman. Since then, neither God nor Man has rested.

Note: Remember this is all in fun. The truth is we love you and we can't live without you. (☺)

BABY PICTURES

The Smiths were unable to conceive children, and decided to use a surrogate father to start their family. On the day the proxy father was to arrive, Mr. Smith kissed his wife and said, "I'm off. The man should be here soon."

Half an hour later, just by chance, a door-to –door baby photographer rang the doorbell, hoping to make a sale. "Good morning madam. I've come to…"

Oh, no need to explain. I've been expecting you, Mrs. Smith cut in. "Really?" the photographer asked. "Well, well! I've made a specialty of babies."

"That's what my husband and I had hoped. Please come in and have a seat." After a moment she asked, blushing, "Well, where do we start?" "Leave everything to me. I usually try two in the bathtub, one on the couch and perhaps a couple on the bed. Sometimes the living room floor is fun too; you can really spread out!"

"Bathtub, living room floor? No wonder it didn't work for Harry and me." "Well, madam, none of us can guarantee a good one every time. But if we try several different positions and I shoot from six or seven angles, I'm sure you'll be pleased with the results."

My, that's a lot of…"gasped Mrs. Smith. "Madam, in my line of work, a man must take his time, I'd love to be in and out in five minutes, but you'd be disappointed with that, I'm sure. "Don't I know it, "Mrs. Smith said quietly?

The photographer opened his briefcase and pulled out a portfolio of his baby pictures. "This was done on the top of a bus." "Oh my god", Mrs. Smith exclaimed, tugging at her handkerchief. "And these twins turned out exceptionally well—-when you consider their mother was so difficult to work with." "She was difficult?" asked Mrs. Smith. "Yes, I'm afraid so. I finally had to take her to the park to get the job done right. People were crowding around four and five deep, pushing to get a good look."

"Four and five deep?" asked Mrs. Smith. Eyes widened in amazement. "Yes," the photographer said. "For more than three hours, too, the mother was constantly squealing and yelling – I could hardly concentrate. Then darkness approached and I began to rush my shots. Finally, when the squirrels began nibbling on my equipment, I just packed it all in."

Mrs. Smith leaned forward. "You mean they actually chewed on your, um…equipment?" "That's right. Well, madam, if you're ready, I'll set up my tripod so that we can get to work." "Tripod?", "Oh yes, I have to use a tripod to rest my Canon on". It's much too big for me to hold very long... Madam? Madam? Are you alright Madam?

BOYS WILL BE BOY'S

A couple had two little boys ages 8 and 10, who were excessively mischievous. They were always getting into trouble and their parents knew that if any mischief occurred in their neighborhood, their sons were probably involved.

The boys' mother heard that a clergyman in town had been successful in disciplining children, so she asked if he would speak with her boys. The clergyman agreed but asked to see them individually. So the mother sent her 8-year-old first, in the morning, with the older boy to see the clergyman in the afternoon.

The clergyman, a huge man with a booming voice, sat the younger boy down and asked him sternly, "Where is god?"

The boy's mouth dropped open, but he made no response, sitting there with his mouth hanging open, wide-eyed. So the clergyman repeated the question in an even sterner tone, "Where is God!!?"

Again the boy made no attempt to answer. So the clergyman raised his voice even more and shook his finger in the boy's face and bellowed, "WHERE IS GOD!?"

The boy screamed and bolted from the room, ran directly home and dove into his closet, slamming the door behind him. When his older brother found him in the closet, he asked, "What happened?"

The younger brother, gasping for breath, replied, "We are in BIG trouble this time, dude. God is missing – and they think WE did it!" (☺)

SENIOR CITIZENS

A group of senior citizens were talking at the breakfast table in a Florida Nursing home. "My arms are so weak I can hardly life this cup of coffee" said one.

"Yes, I know. My cataracts are so bad I can't even see my coffee," replied another.

"I can't turn my head because of the arthritis in my neck," said a third, to which several nodded weakly in agreement.

"My blood pressure pills make me dizzy," another went on. "I guess that's the price we pay for getting old," winced an old man as he slowly shook his head. Then there was a short moment of silence.

"Well, it's not that bad," said one woman cheerfully. "Thank God we can all still drive." (☺)

DEAR ABBY

(Funny Stuff)

Dear Abby:

My husband is a liar and a cheat. He has cheated on me from the beginning, and, when I confront him, he denies everything. What's worse, everyone knows that he cheats on me. It is so humiliating. Also, since he lost his job five years ago, he hasn't even looked for a new one. All he does all day is smoke cigars, cruise around and BS with his buddies while I have to work to pay the bills. Since our daughter went away to college he doesn't even pretend to like me and hints that I may be a lesbian. What should I do?

Signed: Clueless

Dear Clueless:

Grow up and dump him. Good grief, woman. You don't need him anymore. You're a United States Senator from New York. Act like one.

CAR

Bought a new car and returned it to the dealer the next day complaining that I couldn't figure out how the radio worked. The salesman explained that the radio was voice activated. "Watch this!" he said, "Nelson", the radio replied, "Ricky or Willie?" "Willie". He continued and "On the Road Again" came from the speakers. Then he said, "Ray Charles", and in an instant "Georgia on My Mind" replaced Willie Nelson. I drove away happy, and for the next few days, every time I'd say, "Beethoven," I'd get beautiful classical music, and if I said, "Beatles," I'd get one of their awesome songs.

Yesterday, a couple ran a red light and nearly creamed my new car, but I swerved in time to avoid them. I yelled, "Ass Holes!" Immediately the French National Anthem began to play, sung by Jane Fonda and Barbara Streisand, backed up by Michael Moore and the Dixie chicks, with John Kerry on guitar, Al Gore on drums, Dan rather on harmonica, Nancy Pelosi on tambourine, Harry Reid on spoons, Bill Clinton on sax and Ted Kennedy on scotch. Damn, I love this car! (☺)

DON'T YOU WISH YOU COULD JUST SAY...?

- Any similarity between you and a human is purely coincidental!
- Anyone who told you to be yourself couldn't have given you worse advice.
- Are your parents siblings?
- As an outsider, what do you think of the human race?
- Calling you stupid would be an insult to stupid people.
- Did your parents ever ask you to run away from home?
- Do you ever wonder what life would be like if you'd had enough oxygen at birth?
- Do you want people to accept you as you are or do you want them to like you?
- Don't you have a terribly empty feeling – in your skull?
- Do you still love nature, despite what it did to you?
- Go ahead, tell them everything you know. It'll only take 10 seconds.
- Have you considered suing your brains for non-support?
- He has a mind like a steel trap – always closed!
- He is living proof that man can live without a brain!
- He is the kind of a man that you would use as a blueprint to build an idiot.
- He's not stupid; he's possessed by a mentally challenged ghost.
- Here's 20 cents. Call all your friends and bring back some change!
- Hi! I'm a human being! What are you?
- How did you get here? Did someone leave your cage open?

- I'd like to see things from your point of view but I can't seem to get my head that far up my ass.
- I bet your brain feels as good as new, seeing that you've never used it.
- I bet your mother has a loud bark?
- I could make a monkey out of you, but why should I take all the credit?
- I don't consider you a vulture. I consider you something a vulture would eat.
- I don't know what makes you so stupid, but it really works!
- I don't think you are a fool. But then what's MY opinion against thousands of others?
- I hear the only place you're ever invited is outside.
- I hear you were born on a farm. Any more in the litter?
- I heard you got a brain transplant and the brain rejected you!
- I know you are 3 and nobody's fool but maybe someone will adopt you.
- I thought of you all day today. I was at the zoo.
- I would ask you how old you are but I know you can't count that high.
- I'd like to help you out. Which way did you come in?
- I'd like to leave you with one thought…but I'm not sure you have anywhere to put it.
- I'm busy now. Can I ignore you some other time?
- I've seen people like you before, but I had to pay admission!
- If I ever need a brain transplant, I'd choose yours because I'd want a brain that had never been used.
- If ignorance is bliss, you must be the happiest person alive.
- If we were to kill everybody who hates you, it wouldn't be murder; it would be genocide!
- If what you don't know can't hurt you, you are invincible.
- If you stand close enough to him, you can hear the ocean.
- If your brain was chocolate it wouldn't fill an M&M bag.
- Keep talking, someday you'll say something intelligent.
- Learn from your parents' mistakes – use birth control.
- So, a thought crossed your mind? Must have been a long and lonely journey.
- Some day you will find yourself – and wish you hadn't.
- There is no vaccine against stupidity.

EQUAL OPPORTUNITY

Three guys die in an accident and go to heaven. When they get their, St.Peter says, "We only have one rule in heaven. Don't step on the Ducks!"

So they enter heaven and sure enough, there are ducks all over the place. It is almost impossible not to step on a duck and although they try their best to avoid them, the first guy accidentally steps on one.

Along comes St. Peter with the ugliest woman he had ever seen. St.Peter chains them together and says, "Your punishment for stepping on a duck is to spend eternity chained to this ugly woman.

The next day, the second guy steps accidentally on a duck and along comes St.Peter, who doesn't miss a thing, and with him is another extremely ugly woman. He chains them together with the same admonishment as the first guy.

The third guy has observed all this and not wanting to be chained for all eternity to an ugly woman, is very careful where he steps. He manages to go months without stepping on any ducks.

One day St. Peter comes up to him with the most gorgeous woman he had ever laid eyes on a very tall, tanned, curvaceous, sexy blonde. St. Peter chains them together without saying a word.

The guy remarks, "wonder what I did to deserve being chained to you for all eternity? She says, "I don't know about you, but I stepped on a duck."

WELL WHAT DID YOU EXPECT?

Once upon a time, a Sultan was blessed with the birth of a son after years of hoping. The boy immediately became the apple of his father's eye. And he became spoiled beyond imagination.

Just before his son's sixth birthday, the sultan said to him, "Son, I love you very much. Your birthday is coming soon what would you like?" His son replied, "Daddy, I would like to have my own airplane. His father bought him American airlines.

Just before his son's seventh birthday, the sultan sad "Son, you are my pride and joy. What would you want for your birthday? Whatever it is, it's yours." His son replied, "Daddy, I would like a boat." His father bought him the Princess Cruise Line.

Just before his son's eight birthday, the Sultan said, "Son, you bring so much happiness into my life. Anything you want, I shall get it for you." His son replied, "Daddy, I would like to be able to watch cartoons." His father bought him Disney Studios.

Just before his son's ninth birthday, the Sultan said, "Son, you are my life. Your birthday is coming soon. Ask what you wish. I will get it for you". His son, who had grown to love Disney, replied, "Daddy, I would like a Mickey Mouse outfit and a Goofy outfit." His father bought him the Democratic Party and CBS news.

MEN REMEMBER

A woman awakes during the night to find that her husband was not in their bed. She put on her robe and goes downstairs to look for him. She finds him sitting at the kitchen table with a hot cup of coffee in front of him. He appears to be in deep thought, just staring at the wall. She watches as he wiped a tear from his eye and takes a sip of his coffee. "What's the matter, dear," she whispers as she steps into the room. "Why are you down here at this time of the night?"

The husband looks up from his coffee, "Do you remember 20 yeas ago when we were dating, and you were only 16", he asks solemnly. The wife is touched to tears thinking that her husband is so caring and sensitive. "Yes I do!" She replies.

The husband paused. The words were not coming easily. "Do you remember when your father caught us in the back seat of my car making love"? "Yes, I remember" said the wife, lowering herself into a chair beside him.

The husband continued. "Do you remember when he shoved the shotgun in my face and said, "Either you marry my daughter, or I will send you to jail for 20 years". "I remember that too", she replied softly.

He wiped another tear from his cheek and said…"I would have gotten out today."

MEN

A man wanted to get married. He was having trouble choosing among three likely candidates. He gives each woman a present of $5,000 and watches to see what they do with the money.

The first does a total make over. She goes to a fancy beauty salon gets her hair done, new make up and buys several new outfits and dresses up very nicely for the man. She tells him that she had done this to be more attractive for him because she loves him so much. The man was impressed.

The second goes shopping to buy the man gifts. She gets him a new set of golf clubs, some new gizmos for his computer, and some expensive clothes. As she presents these gifts, she tells him that she has spent all the money on him because she loves him so much. Again, the man is impressed.

The third invests the money in the stock market. She earns several times the $5,000. She gives him back his $5,000 and reinvests the remainder in a joint account. She tells him that she wants to save for their future because she loves him so much. Obviously, the man was impressed.

The man thought for a long time about what each woman had done with the money he'd given them. Then, he married the one with the biggest boobs. Men are like that, you know.

There is more money being spent on Brest implants and Viagra today than on Alzheimer's research.

The Moral is: This means that by 2040, there should be a large elderly population with perky boobs and huge erections and absolutely no recollection of what to do with them. (☺)

OLD MEN

A senior citizen goes in for his yearly physical with his wife tagging along. When the doctor enters the examination room he says, "I will need a urine sample, a stool sample, and a sperm sample." The man, being hard of hearing, turns to his wife and asks, "What did he say?" The wife yells back at him, "GIVE HIM YOUR UNDERWEAR!"

OLDER PEOPLE

Jacob, age 92, and Rebecca, age 89, living in Florida, are all excited about their decision to get married. They go for a stroll to discuss the wedding, and on the way they pass a drugstore. Jacob suggests they go in. He addresses the man behind the counter: "Are you the owner?" The Pharmacist answers, "Yes."

Jacob : "We're about to get married. Do you sell heart medications?" Pharmacist answers, "Of course we do."

Jacob : "How about medicine for circulation?" Pharmacist: "All kinds."

Jacob : "Medicine for rheumatism and scoliosis? Pharmacist: Definitely."

Jacob : "How about Viagra? Pharmacist: "Of course."

Jacob : "Medicine for memory problems, arthritis, Jaundice"? Pharmacist: "Yes, a large variety. The works."

Jacob : "What about vitamins, sleeping pills, Geritol, antidotes for Parkinson's disease?" Pharmacist: "Absolutely."

Jacob : "You sell wheelchairs and walkers?" Pharmacist: "All speeds and sizes."

Jacob : "We'd like to use this store as our Bridal Registry".

KIDS DO LISTEN

Hillary and Chelsea: After Chelsea returned from a date, Hillary asked her if she had a good time. Chelsea said she had a wonderful time and she thinks she's in love. Hillary said, "You didn't have sex, did you?" A long silence and then Chelsea said, "Not according to Dad."

SOME REALLY DUMB STUFF TO THINK ABOUT

(When you are really, really bored)

- Can you cry under water?
- How important does a person have to be before they are considered assassinated instead of just murdered?
- Why do you have to "put your two cents in"…but it's only a "penny for your thoughts"? Where's that extra penny going to?
- Once you're in heaven, do you get stuck wearing the clothes you were buried in for eternity?
- Why does a round pizza come in a square box?
- What disease did cured ham actually have?
- How is it that we put man on the moon before we figured out it would be a good idea to put wheels on luggage?
- Why is it that people say they "Slept like a baby" when babies wake up like every two hours?
- If a deaf person has to go to court, is it still called a hearing?
- Why are you IN a movie, but you're ON TV?
- Why do people pay to go up tall buildings and then put money in binoculars to look at things on the ground?
- Why do doctors leave the room while you change? They're going to see you naked anyway.
- Why is "bra" singular and "panties" plural?
- Why do toasters always have a setting that burns the toast to a horrible crisp, which no decent human being would eat?

- Can a hearse carrying a corpse drive in the carpool lane?
- If the professor of Gilligan's Island can make a radio out of a coconut, why can't he fix a hole in a boat?
- If Wiley E. Coyote had enough money to buy all that ACME stuff, why didn't he just buy dinner?
- If corn oil is made from corn, and vegetable oil is made from vegetables, what is baby oil made from?
- Do the Alphabet song and Twinkle, Twinkle Little Star have the same tune?
- Why did you just try singing the two songs above?
- Why do they call it an asteroid when it's outside the hemisphere, but call it a hemorrhoid when it's in your butt?

STATE FAIR

Morris and his wife Esther went to the state fair every year, and every year Morris would say, "Esther, I'd like to ride in that helicopter." Esther always replied, "I know Morris, but that helicopter ride is $50 and $50 is $50."

One year Esther and Morris went to the fair, and Morris said; "Esther I'm 85 years old. If I don't ride that helicopter, I might never get another chance." Esther replied, "Morris that helicopter is $50 and $50 is $50."

The pilot over heard the couple and said, "Folks I'll make you a deal. I'll take the both of you for a ride. If you can stay quiet for the entire ride and not say a word I won't charge you! But, if you say one word, its $50".

Morris and Esther agreed and up they went. The pilot did all kinds of fancy maneuvers, but not a word was heard. He did his dare devil, tricks over and over again, but still not a word, when they landed the pilot turned to Morris and said: "By golly, I did everything I could to get you to yell out, but you didn't, I'm impressed!"

Morris replied, "Well I was going to say something when Esther fell out, but $50 is $50.

LAWYER

A very successful lawyer parked his brand new Lexus in front of the office, ready to show it off to his colleagues. As he got out, a truck came along too close to the curb and completely tore off the driver's door. Fortunately, a cop in a police car was close enough to see the accident and pulled up behind the Lexus, his lights flashing. But, before the cop had a chance to ask any questions, the lawyer started screaming hysterically about how his Lexus, which he had just picked up the day before, was now completely ruined and would never be the same, no matter how the body shop tried to make it new again. After the lawyer finally wound down from his rant, the cop shook his head in disgust and disbelief.

"I can't believe how materialistic you lawyers are," he said. "You are so focused on your possessions that you neglect the most important things in life." "How can you say such a thing?" asked the lawyer. The cop replied. "Don't you even realize that your left arm is missing? It got ripped off when the truck hit you!!!" "OH MY GOD!" screamed the lawyer. (Scroll down)

✻
✻
✻
✻
✻
"MY ROLEX!"

THE BLIND MAN

A blind man makes his way to a bar stool and orders a drink. After sitting there for awhile, he yells to the bartender, "Hay, you wanna hear a blonde joke?"

The bar immediately falls absolutely quiet. In a very deep, husky voice, the woman next to him says, "Before you tell that joke, sir, I think it is only fair, given that you are blind, that you should know five things:

1. The bartender is a blonde girl with a baseball bat.
2. The bouncer is a blonde "Biker girl."
3. I'm a 6-foot tall 185-pound woman with a black belt in Karate.
4. The woman sitting next to me is a blonde and a professional Weightlifter
5. The lady to your right is blonde and a professional Wrestler.

Now, think about it seriously, Mister. Do you still wanna tell that blonde joke?

The blind man thinks for a second, shakes his head and mutters, "NAH, not if I'm gonna have to explain it five times."(☺)

THEY WALK AMONG US

1. While looking at a house, my brother asked the real estate agent which direction was north because, he explained, he didn't want the sun waking him up every morning. She asked. "Does the sun rise in the North?" When my brother explained that the sun rises in the East, and has for EVER, she shook her head and said, "Oh, I don't keep up with that stuff." They Walk Among Us!

2. I used to work in technical support for a 24/7 call center. One day I got a call from an individual who asked what hours the call center was open.
   I told him, "The number you dialed is open 24 hours a day, 7 days a week." He responded, "Is that Eastern or Pacific time?" Wanting to end the call quickly, I said, "Uh, Pacific." They Walk Among Us!

3. My colleague and I were eating our lunch in our cafeteria, when we overheard one of the administrative assistants talking about the sunburn she got on her weekend drive to the shore. She drove down in a convertible, but "didn't think she'd get sunburned because the car was moving." They Walk Among Us!

4. My friend has a lifesaving tool in her car it's designed to cut through a seat belt if she gets trapped. She keeps it in the trunk. They Walk Among Us!

5. I was hanging out with a friend when we saw a woman with a nose ring attached to an earring by a chain. My friend said, "Wouldn't

the chain rip out every time she turned her head?" I explained that a person's nose and ear remain the same distance apart no matter which way the head is turned. Sometimes They Run Among Us!

6. I couldn't find my luggage at the airport baggage area. So I went to the lost luggage office and told the woman there that my bags never showed up. She smiled and told me not to worry because she was a trained professional and I was in good hands, "Now," she asked me, "has your plane arrived yet?" They Walk Among Us!

7. While working at a pizza parlor I observed a man ordering a small pizza to go. He appeared to be alone and the cook asked him if he would like it cut into 4 pieces or 6. He thought about it for some time before responding.
"Just cut it into 4 pieces: I don't think I'm hungry enough to eat 6 pieces. Yep, they Walk Among us & they reproduce.

WHEN HEAVEN CALLS

An engineer dies and reports to the pearly gates. St. Peter checks his dossier and say, "Ah, you're an engineer – you're in the wrong place." So, the engineer reports to the gates of hell and is let in.

Pretty soon, the engineer gets dissatisfied with the level of comfort in hell, and starts designing and building improvements. After a while, they've got air conditioning and flush toilets and escalators, and the engineer is a pretty popular guy.

One day, God calls Satan up on the telephone and says with a sneer, "So, how's it going down there in hell?"

Satan replies, "Hey, things are going great. We've got air conditioning and flush toilets and escalators, and there's no telling what this engineer is going to come up with next."

God replies, "What??? You've got an engineer? That's a mistake – he should never have gotten down there; send him up here."

Satan says, "No way." I like having an engineer on the staff, and I'm keeping him." God says, "Send him back up here or I'll sue."

Satan laughs uproariously and answers, "Yeah, right. And just where are YOU going to get a lawyer?" (☺)

THE FOLLOWER

A mom was concerned about her kindergarten son walking to school since he didn't want his mother to walk with him. She had an idea of how to handle it. She asked her good friend if she would follow him to school, staying at a distance so he wouldn't notice her.

The friend said since she was up early with her toddler anyway, it would be a good way for them to get some exercise, so she agreed. The next school day, the friend and her little girl set out following Timmy as he walked to school with another neighborhood boy he knew. She did this for the whole week.

As the boys walked along, kicking stones and chatting, Timmy's little friend noticed the same lady following them. Finally he said to Timmy, "Have you noticed the lady following us to school all week? Do you know her?"

Timmy nonchalantly replied, "Yes, I know who she is. The friend said, "Well, who is she? "That's just Shirley Goodnest and her daughter Marcy," replied Timmy.

"Shirley Goodnest? Who the heck is she and why is she following us?" asked his friend.

"Well," Timmy explained, "every night my mom has me say the 23rd Psalm with my prayers because she worries about me so much. And in the Psalm, it says, "Shirley Goodnest and Marcy shall follow me all the days of my life" so I guess I'll just have to get used to it!" May Shirley Goodnest and Marcy be with you today and always.

WISCONSIN

Recently a routine police patrol parked outside a bar in Madison, WI. After last call the officer noticed a man leaving the bar so intoxicated that he could barely walk. The man stumbled around the parking lot for a few minutes, with the officer quietly observing.

After what seemed an eternity and trying his keys on five different vehicles, the man managed to find his car which he fell into. He sat there for a few minutes as a number of other patrons left the bar and drove off. Finally he started the car, switched the wipers on and off (it was a fine, dry summer night) flicked the blinkers on, then off a couple of times, honked the horn and then switched on the lights. He moved the vehicle forward a few inches, reversed a little and then remained still for a few more minutes as some more of the other patron vehicles left. At last, the parking lot was empty; he pulled out of the parking lot and started to drive slowly down the road.

The police officer, having patiently waited all this time, now started up the patrol car, put on the flashing lights, and promptly pulled the man over and carried out a breathalyzer test. To his amazement the breathalyzer indicated no evidence of the man having consumed any alcohol at all!

Dumbfounded, the officer said, "I'll have to ask you to accompany me to the police station. This breathalyzer equipment must be broken. "I doubt it," said the truly proud Wisconsinite. "Tonight I'm the designated decoy."

THE WORK PLACE

(Moral in every lesson)

Lesson 1.

A man is getting into the shower just as his wife is finishing up her shower, when the doorbell rings. The wife quickly wraps herself in a towel and runs downstairs. When she opens the door, there stands Bob, the next-door neighbor. Before she says a word, Bob says, "I'll give you $800 to drop that towel." After thinking for a moment, the woman drops her towel and stands naked in front of Bob, after a few seconds, Bob hands her $800 and leaves. The woman wraps back up in the towel and goes back upstairs. When she gets to the bathroom, her husband asks, "Who was that?" "It was Bob the next door neighbor." She replies. "Great," the husband says. "Did he say anything about the $800 he owes me?"

(Moral of the story ☺)

If you share critical information pertaining to credit and risk with your shareholders in time, you may be in a position to prevent avoidable exposure.

Lesson 2.

A sales rep, an administration clerk, and the manager are walking to lunch when they find an antique oil lamp. They rub it and a Genie comes out. The Genie says, "I'll give each of you just one wish." "Me first! Me first" says the admin clerk. "I want to be in the Bahamas, driving a speedboat, without a care in the world." Puff! She's gone. "Me next! Me next!" says the sales rep. "I want to be in Hawaii, relaxing on the beach with my personal masseuse, an endless supply of Pina Coladas and the love of my life." Puff! He's gone. "OK, you're up." The Genie says to the manager. The manager says, "I want those two back in the office after lunch."

(Moral of the Story ☺)

Always let your boss have the first say.

Lesson 3.

An eagle was sitting on a tree resting, doing nothing. A small rabbit saw the eagle and asked him, "Can I also sit like you and do nothing?" The eagle answered: "Sure, why not." So, the rabbit sat on the ground below the eagle and rested. All of a sudden, a fox appeared, jumped on the rabbit and ate it.

(Moral of the story)

To be sitting and doing nothing, you must be sitting very, very high up.

Lesson 4.

A turkey was chatting with a bull. "I'd love to be able to get to the tip of that tree, sighed the turkey, "but I haven't got the energy." "Well, why don't you nibble on some of my droppings?" replied the bull. They're packed with nutrients." The turkey pecked at a lump of dung, and found it actually gave him enough strength to reach the lowest branch of the tree. The next day, after eating some more dung, he reached the second branch. Finally after a fourth night, the turkey was proudly perched at the top of the tree. He was promptly spotted by a farmer, who shot him out of the tree.

(Moral of the story ☺)

Bull crap might get you to the top, but it won't keep you there.

Lesson 5.

A little bird was flying south for the winter. It was so cold the bird froze and fell to the ground into a large field. While he was lying there, a cow came by and dropped some dung on him. As the frozen bird lay there in the pile of cow dung, he began to realize how warm he was. The dung was actually thawing him out! He lay there all warm and happy, and soon began to sing for joy. A passing cat heard the bird singing and came to investigate. Following the sound, the cat discovered the bird under the pile of cow dung, and promptly dug him out and ate him.

(Morals of the story ☺)

    a. Not everyone who craps on you is your enemy.
    b. Not everyone who gets you out of crap is your friend.
    c. And when you're in deep crap, it's best to keep your mouth shut!

CHRISTMAS GOLF

Four old-timers were playing their weekly game of golf, and one remarked how nice it would be to wake up on Christmas morning, roll out of bed and without an argument go directly to the golf course, meet his buddies and play a round of gold.

His buddies all chimed in and said, "Let's do it! We'll make it a priority, figure out a way and meet her early Christmas morning."

Months later, that special morning arrives, and there they are on the golf course.

The first guy says, "Boy this game cost me a fortune! I bought my wife such a diamond ring that she can't take her eyes off it."

The second guy says, "I spent a ton, too. My wife is at home planning the cruise I gave her. She was up to her eyeballs in brochures."

The third guy says. "Well my wife is at home admiring her new car, reading the manual."

They all turned to the last guy in the group who is staring at them like they have lost their minds.

"I can't believe you all went to such expense for this golf game. I slapped my wife on the butt and said, "Well, babe, Merry Christmas! It's a great morning for sex or golf" and she said, "Take a sweater…""

GREAT TRUTHS

Great truths that little children have learned:

1. No matter how hard you try, you can't baptize cats.
2. When your Mom is mad at your Dad, don't let her brush your hair.
3. If your sister hits you, don't hit her back. They always catch the second person.
4. Never ask your 3 year old brother to hold a tomato.
5. You can't trust dogs to watch your food
6. Don't sneeze when someone is cutting your hair.
7. Never hold a dust-Buster and a cat at the same time.
8. You can't hide a piece of broccoli in a glass of milk.
9. Don't wear polka-dot underwear under white shorts.
10. The best place to be when you're sad is Grandpa's lap.

Great truths that Adults have learned:

1. Raising teenagers is like nailing Jell-O to a tree.
2. Wrinkles don't hurt.
3. Families are like fudge...mostly sweet, with a few nuts.
4. Today's mighty oak is just yesterday's nut that held its ground.
5. Laughing is good exercise. It's like jogging on the inside.
6. Middle age is when you choose your cereal for the fiber, not the toy.

Great truths that older people have learned:

1. Growing up is mandatory; growing old is optional.
2. Forget the health food. We need all the preservatives we can get.
3. When you fall down, you wonder what else you can do while you're down there.
4. You're getting old when you get the same sensations from a rocking chair that you once got from a roller coaster.
5. It's frustrating when you know all the answers but nobody bothers to ask you the questions.
6. Time may be a great healer, but it's a lousy beautician.
7. Wisdom comes with age, but sometimes age comes alone.

FOR PEOPLE 50 YEARS OR OLDER & ESPECIALLY FOR THE YOUTH

1. I was born before television
2. Before penicillin
3. Before polio shots
4. Before frozen foods
5. Before Xerox
6. Before contact lenses
7. Before Frisbees
8. Before the pill
9. Before radar
10. Before credit cards
11. Before laser beams
12. Before Ball-point pens
13. Before pantyhose
14. Before dishwashers
15. Before clothes dryers
16. Before electric blankets
17. Before air conditioners
18. Before man walked on the moon
19. Before computer-dating
20. Before dual careers
21. Before daycare centers
22. Before group therapy

23. Before FM radio
24. Before the Tape deck
25. Before CDs
26. Before typewriters
27. Before yogurt
28. Before guys wearing earrings
29. Before Pizza Hut
30. Before Mc Donald's
31. Before instant coffee
☺ Do you think this is enough? ☺

ACTUAL WRITINGS ON HOSPITAL CHARTS

1. She has no rigors or shaking chills, but her husband states she was very hot in bed last night.
2. Patient has chest pain if she lies on her left side for over a year.
3. On the second day the knee was better, and on the third day it disappeared.
4. The patient has been depressed since she began seeing me in 1993.
5. Discharge status: Alive but without my permission.
6. Healthy appearing decrepit 69 year old male, mentally alert but forgetful.
7. The patient refused autopsy.
8. The patient has no previous history of suicides.
9. The patient has left white blood cells at another hospital.
10. Patient's medical history has been remarkably insignificant with only a 40 pound weight gain in the past three days.
11. Patient had waffles for breakfast and anorexia for lunch.
12. She is numb from her toes down.
13. While in ER, she was examined, X-rated and sent home.
14. The skin was moist and dry.
15. Occasional, constant infrequent headaches.
16. Patient was alert and unresponsive.
17. Rectal examination revealed a normal size thyroid.
18. She stated that she had been constipated for most of her life, until she got a divorce.

19. I saw your patient today, who is still under our car for physical therapy.
20. Both breast are equal and reactive to light and accommodation.
21. Examination of genitalia reveals that he is circus sized.
22. The lab test indicated abnormal lover function.
23. The patient was to have a bowel resection. However, he took a job as a stock broker instead.
24. Skin; somewhat pale but present.
25. The pelvic exam will be done later on the floor.
26. Patient was seen in consultation by Dr. Blank, who felt we should sit on the abdomen and I agree.
27. Large brown stool ambulating in the hall.
28. Patient has two teenage children, but no other
29. The patient is tearful and crying constantly. She also appears to be depressed.

DID YOU EVER WONDER WHY?

- Why do we press harder on a remote control when we know the batteries are getting weak?
- Why do banks charge a fee on "Insufficient Funds" when they know there is not enough?
- Why does someone believe you when you say there are four billion stars, but check when you say the paint is wet?
- Why doesn't glue stick to the bottle?
- Why do they use sterilized needles for death by lethal injections?
- Why doesn't Tarzan have a beard?
- Why does superman stop bullets with his chest, but duck when you throw a revolver at him?
- Why do Kamikaze pilots wear helmets?
- Whose idea was it to put an "S" in the word "Lisp"?
- If people evolved from apes, why are there still apes?
- Why is it that no matter what color bubble bath you use the bubbles are always white?
- Is there ever a day that mattresses are not on sale?
- Why do people constantly return to the refrigerator with hopes that something new to eat will have materialized?
- Why do people keep running over a string a dozen times with their vacuum cleaner, then reach down, pick it up, examine it, then put it down to give the vacuum one more chance?
- Why is it that no plastic bag will open from the end you first try?
- How do those dead bugs get into those enclosed light fixtures?

- Why is it that whenever you attempt to catch something that's falling off the table you always manage to knock something else over?
- In winter why do we try to keep the house as warm as it was in summer when we complained about the heat?
- Why do you never hear father-in-law jokes?

DA VINCI CODE

Written across the wall of the cave were the following symbols;
It was considered a unique find and the writings were said to be at least
three thousand years old!

The piece of stone was removed, brought to the museum, and
archaeologists from around the world came to study the ancient
symbols. They held a huge meeting after months of conferences to
discuss the meaning of the markings.

The President of the society pointed to the first drawing and said:
"This is a woman. We can see these people held women in high esteem.
You can also tell they were intelligent, as the next symbol is a donkey,
so they were smart enough to have animals help them till the soil. The
next drawing is a shovel, which means they had tools to help them."

Even further proof of their high intelligence is the fish which means
that if a famine hit the earth and food didn't grow, they would seek
food from the sea. The last symbol appears to be the Star of David
which means they were evidently Hebrews. The audience applauded
enthusiastically.

Then a little old Jewish man stood up in the back of the room and
said, "**IDIOTS**, Hebrew is read from right to left. It says: "Holy
Mackerel Dig the ass on that chick." (☺)

TOP 35 OXYMORON'S (☺)

35. State worker
34. Legally drunk
33. Exact estimate
32. Act naturally
31. Found missing
30. Resident alien
29. Genuine imitation
28. Airline food
27. Good grief
26. Government organization
25. Sanitary landfill
24. Alone together
23. Small crowd
22. Business ethics
21. Soft rock
20. Amtrak schedule
19. Military intelligence
18. Sweet sorrow
17. Compassionate conservative
16. "Now, then..."
15. Passive aggression
14. Clearly misunderstood
13. Peace force

12. Extinct life
11. Plastic glasses
10. Terribly pleased
9. Computer security
8. Political science
7. Tight slacks
6. Definite maybe
5. Pretty ugly
4. Rap music
3. Working vacation
2. Religious tolerance
And the #1 Oxymoron... <u>Microsoft Works</u> (☺)

GOOD BAPTIST

A Baptist minister was seated next to a Marine on a flight to Huntsville, Alabama. After the plane was air borne, drink orders were taken. The marine asked for a whiskey and soda, which was brought and placed before him. The flight attendant then asked the minister if he would like a drink. He replied in disgust. "I'd rather be savagely raped by brazen whores than let liquor touch my lips." The Marine then handed his drink back to the attendant and said, "Me too. I didn't know we had a choice." (☺ (☺ (☺)

CISSY & GEORGE

(Senior Humor)

Cissy and George are lying in bed one morning, having just awakened from a good night's sleep. George takes Cissy's hand and she responds, "Don't touch me." "Why not?" George asks. She answers back, "Because I'm dead." Then George says, "What are you talking about? We're both lying here in bed together and talking to one another." She says, "No, I'm definitely dead." He insists, "You're not dead. What in the world makes you think you're dead?" Cissy responds, "Because I woke up this morning and nothing hurts."

THE BEST HEADLINES OF 2003

- Something Went Wrong in Jet Crash, Expert Say's
- Police begin Campaign to Run down Jaywalkers
- Iraqi Head Seeks arms
- Panda Mating Fails; Veterinarian Takes Over
- Teacher Strikes Idle Kids
- Miners Refuse to work after Death
- Juvenile court to Try Shooting Defendant
- War dims Hope for Peace
- Cold wave Lined to Temperatures
- Enfield (London) couple Slain; Police Suspect Homicide
- Red Tape Holds Up New Bridges
- Man Struck By Lightning Faces Battery Charge
- New Study of Obesity Looks for Larger Test Group
- Astronaut takes Blame for Gas in Spacecraft
- Kids Make Nutritious Snacks
- Chef Throws his Heart into Helping Feed Needy
- Local High School Dropouts Cut in Half
- Hospitals are sued by 7 Foot Doctors
- **And the winner is** – Typhoon Rips Through Cemetery; Hundreds Dead.

THE PREACHERS SON

An old country preacher had a teenage son, and it was getting time the boy should give some thought to choosing a profession. Like many young men, the boy didn't really know what he wanted to do, and he didn't seem too concerned about it. One day, while the boy was away at school, his father decided to try an experiment. He went into the boy's room and placed on his study table four objects (1) a Bible (2) a Silver dollar (3) a bottle of whisky & (4) a Playboy magazine. I'll just hide behind the door, "the old preacher said to himself," and when he comes home from school this afternoon, I'll see which object he picks up. If it's the Bible, he's going to be a preacher like me, and what a blessing that would be! If he picks up the dollar, he's going to be a businessman, and that would be okay, too. But if he picks up the bottle, he's going to be a no-good drunkard, and, Lord, what a shame that would be. And worst of all, if he picks up the magazine he's going to be a skirt-chasing' bum."

The old man waited anxiously, and soon heard his son's footsteps as he entered the house whistling and headed for his room. The boy tossed his books on the bed, and as he turned to leave the room he spotted the objects on the table. With curiosity in his eyes, he walked over to inspect them. Finally, he picked up the Bible and placed it under his arm. He picked up the silver dollar and dropped it into his pocket. He uncorked the bottle and took a big drink while he admired this month's Centerfold. "Lord have mercy." The old preacher disgustedly whispered, "He's going to be a Senator!"

LANGUAGE BARRIER

A polish man moved to the USA and married an American girl. Although his English was far from perfect, they got along very well.

One day he rushed into a lawyer's office and asked him if he could arrange a divorce for him. The lawyer said that getting a divorce would depend on the circumstances, and asked him the following questions:

Have you any grounds? Yes, an acre and half and nice little home. No, I mean what is the foundation of this case? It made of concrete.

I don't think you understand. Does either of you have a real grudge? No, we have carport, and not need one. I mean. What are your relations like? All my relations still in Poland.

Is there any infidelity in your marriage? We have hi-fidelity stereo and good DVD player.

Does your wife beat you up? No, I always up before her.

Why do you want this divorce? She going to kill me. What makes you think that? I got proof.

What kind of proof? She going to poison me. She buy a bottle at drugstore and put on shelf in bathroom. I can read, and it say; "Polish Remover."

Note: They are still married. (☺)

OLE'S ANSWER (☺)

Ole had a car accident. In court, the trucking company's lawyer was questioning Ole. Didn't you say, at the scene of the accident, "I'm fine."? Asked the lawyer.

Ole responded, "Val, I'll tell you vat happened. I had just loaded my favorite mule Bessie into the..." I didn't ask for any details." The lawyer interrupted. "Just answer the question. Did you not say, at the scene of the accident I'm fine!"?

Ole said, "Vell, I had just got Bessie into the trailer and I was driving down the road..." The lawyer interrupted again and said, "Judge, I am trying to establish the fact that, at the scene of the accident, this man told the Highway Patrolman on duty that he was just fine. Now several weeks after the accident he is trying to sue my client. I believe he is a fraud. Please tell him to simply answer the question."

By this time, the judge was fairly interested in Ole's answer and said to the lawyer, "I'd like to hear what he has to say about his favorite mule, Bessie."

Ole thanked the judge and proceeded. "Vell as I vas saying. I had just loaded Bessie, my favorite mule, into the trailer and vas driving her down the highway ven this huge semi-truck and trailer ran the stop sign and smacked my truck right in the side. I vas thrown into one ditch and Bessie vas thrown into the other. I vas hurting real bad and didn't vant to move.

However, I could hear Bessie moaning and groaning. I knew she was in terrible shape just by her groans. Shortly after the accident a Highway Patrolman came on the scene. He could hear Bessie moaning and groaning so he went over to her. After he looked at her, and saw her fatal condition, he took out his gun and shot her between the eyes. Then the patrolman came across the road, gun still in hand, looked at me and said, "How are you feeling?"

"Now vat the HELL would you say?" (☺)

JUST TRIVIA & MORE TRIVIA (☺)

- The first couple to be shown in bed together on prime time TV was Fred & Wilma Flinstone.
- Every day more money is printed for Monopoly than the US Treasury.
- Men can read smaller print than women can; women can hear better.
- Coca-Cola was originally green.
- The state with the highest percentage of people who walk to work: Alaska.
- The percentage of Africa that is wilderness: 28%
- The percentage of North America that is wilderness: 38%
- The cost of raising a medium-size dog to the age of eleven: $6,400
- The average number of people airborne over the US and given hour: 61,000
- Intelligent people have more zinc and copper in their hair.
- The world's youngest parents were 8 and 9 and lived in China in 1910.
- The youngest pope was 11 years old.
- The first novel ever written on a typewriter: Tom sawyer.
- Those San Francisco Cable cars are the only mobile National Monuments.
- Each king in a deck of playing cards represents a great king from history: <u>Spades</u> – King David <u>Hearts</u>-Charlemagne <u>Clubs</u>-Alexander, the great <u>Diamonds</u>-Julius Caesar.

- 111,111,111 X 111,111,111 = 12,345,678,987,654,321
- A statue in the park of a person on a horse with both front legs in the air, that person died in battle. If the horse has one front leg in the air that person died as a result of wounds received in battle. If the horse has all four legs on the ground, that person died of natural causes.
- "I am." Is the shortest complete sentence in the English language.
- Hershey's Kisses are called that because the machine that makes them looks like it's kissing the conveyor belt.
- (Q.) Half of all Americans live within 50 miles of what? (A.) Their birthplace.
- (Q.) What is the most popular boat name? (A.) Obsession
- (Q.) If you were to spell out numbers, how far would you have to go until you would find the letter "A"? (A.) One thousand
- (Q.) What do bulletproof vests, fire escapes, windshield wipers, and laser printers all have in common? (A.) All invented by women.
- (Q.) What is the only food that doesn't spoil? (A.) Honey
- (Q.) There are more collect calls on this day than any other day of the year? (A.) Father's Day
- (Q.) What trivia fact about Mel Blanc (voice of Bugs Bunny) is the most ironic? (A.) He was allergic to carrots.
- (Q.) what is an activity performed by 40% of all people at a party? (A.) Snoop in your medicine cabinet.

COWBOY STORY

A modern day cowboy has spent many days crossing the desert without water. His horse has already died of thirst. He's crawling through the sands, certain that he has breathed his last, when all of a sudden; he sees an object sticking out of the sand several yards ahead of him. He crawls to the object, pulls it out of the sand, and discovers what looks to be an old brief case. He opens it and out pops a genie. But this is no ordinary genie. She is wearing an Internal Revenue Service ID badge and a dull grey dress. There's a calculator in her pocketbook. She has a pencil tucked behind her ear.

"Well, cowboy," says the genie..."You know how it works. You have three wishes." "I'm not falling for this," Says the cowboy. "I'm not going to trust an IRS auditor."

"What do you have to lose? You've got no transportation and it looks like you're a goner anyway!"

The cowboy thinks about this for a minute and decides that the genie is right. "OK, I wish I were in a lush oasis with plenty of food and drink."

POOF The cowboy finds himself in the most beautiful oasis he has ever seen. And he is surrounded with jugs of wine and platters of delicacies.

"OK, cowpoke, what's your second wish."

"My second wish is that I was rich beyond my wildest dreams." ***POOF*** He finds himself surrounded by treasure chests filled with rare gold coins and precious gems.

"OK, cowpuncher, you have just one more wish. Better make it a good one!"

After thinking for a few minutes, the cowboy says…"I wish that no matter where I go, beautiful women will want and need me."
POOF He is turned into a tampon.

The moral of the story: If the government offers you anything, there's going to be a string attached. (☺) ☹

CHILDREN AND THE CHURCH

1. A little boy was attending his first wedding. After the service, his cousin asked him, "How many women can a man marry?" "Sixteen," the boy responded. His cousin was amazed that he had an answer so quickly. "How do you know that?" "Easy." The little boy said. "All you have to do is add it up, like the pastor said, 4 better, 4 worse, 4 richer, 4 poorer."

2. After a church service on Sunday morning, a young boy suddenly announced to his mother, "Mom, I've decided to become a minister when I grow up." "That's okay with us, but what made you decide that?" "Well," said the little boy, "I have to go to church on Sunday anyway, and I figure it will be more fun to stand up and yell, than to sit and listen

3. A 6-year-old was overheard reciting the Lord's Prayer at a church service, "And forgive us our trash passes, as we forgive those who passed trash against us."

4. A boy was watching his father, a pastor, write a sermon. "How do you know what to say?" he asked. "Why, God tells me." "Oh, then why do you keep crossing things out?"

5. A little girl became restless as the preacher's sermon dragged on and on. Finally, she leaned over to her mother and whispered, "Mommy, if we give him the money now, will he let us go?"

6. Ms. Terri asked her Sunday School Class to draw pictures of their favorite bible stories. She was puzzled by Kyle's picture, which showed four people on an airplane, so she asked him which story it was meant to represent. "The Flight to Egypt," was his reply. Pointing at each figure, Ms. Terri said, "That must be Mary, Joseph, and Baby Jesus. But who's the fourth person?" "Oh, that's Pontius – the pilot!"

7. The Sunday School Teacher asks, "Now, Johnny, tell me frankly do you say prayers before eating?" "No sir," little Johnny replies, I don't have to. My mom is a good cook.

8. **I love this one**. A little girl was sitting on her grandfather's lap as he read her a bedtime story. From time to time, she would take her eyes off the book and reach up to touch his wrinkled cheek. She was alternately stroking her own cheek, then his again. Finally she spoke up, "Grandpa, did God make you?" "Yes, sweetheart," he answered, "God made me a long time ago." "Oh," she paused, "Grandpa, did god make me too?" "Yes, indeed, honey," he said, "God made you just a little while ago." Feeling their respective faces again, she observed, "God's getting better at it, isn't he?"

FLIGHT CHATTER

- On a lengthy evening Air Canada flight with a somewhat "senior" flight attendant crew, the pilot said, "Ladies and Gentlemen, we've reached cruising altitude and will be turning down the cabin lights. This is for your comfort and to enhance the appearance of your flight attendants." (Ouch! ☺)

- Upon landing, a Westjet stewardess was heard to say: "Please be sure to take all of your belongings. If you're going to leave anything, please make sure it's something we'd like to have."

- Also from Westjet: "There may be 50 ways to leave your lover, but there are only 4 ways out of this airplane. So pay attention!"

- "Thank you for flying Delta Business express. We hope you enjoyed giving us the business as much as we enjoyed taking you for a ride."

- As the Continental plane landed and was coming to a stop at La Guardia, a lone voice came over the loudspeaker; "Whoa, big fella. WHOA!"

- After a particular rough landing during a thunderstorm in Memphis, a flight attendant on a Northwest flight announced: "Please take care when opening the overhead compartments because, after a landing like that, sure as hell everything has shifted."

- From a southwest Airlines flight crew member; "Welcome aboard southwest flight 245 to Tampa. To operate your seat belt, insert the metal tab into the buckle, and pull tight. It works just like every other seat belt; and, if you don't know how to operate one, you probably shouldn't be out in public unsupervised."

- In the event of a sudden loss of cabin pressure, masks will descent from the ceiling. Stop screaming, grab the mask, and pull it over your face. If you have a small child traveling with you, secure your mask before assisting with theirs. If you are traveling with more than one small child, pick your favorite.

- The captain's dulcet tones droned over the plane's speaker; "Weather at our destination is 50 degrees with some broken clouds, but we'll try to have them fixed before we arrive. Thank you, and remember, nobody loves you, or your money, more than southwest Airlines.

- "Your seat cushions can be used for flotation. In the event of an emergency water landing, please use them to paddle to shore and feel free to take them home with our compliments.

- "Should the cabin lose pressure, oxygen masks are in the overhead area. Please place the bag over your own mouth and nose before assisting children or other adults acting like children."

- "As you exit the plane, make sure to gather all of your belongings. Anything left behind will be distributed equally among the flight attendants. Please do not leave children or spouses."

- And from the pilot during his welcome message: "Delta airlines is pleased to have some of the best flight attendants in the industry. Unfortunately, none of them are on this flight!"

- Heard from a flight attendant on a Westjet airlines flight just after a very hard landing in Edmonton, Alberta: "That was quite a bump, and I know what you're all thinking…I'm here to tell you it wasn't the airline's fault, it wasn't the pilot's fault, it wasn't the flight attendant's fault…It was the asphalt."

- Overheard on an American Airlines flight into Amarillo, Texas, on a particularly windy and bumpy day; During the final approach, the captain was really having to fight it after an extremely hard landing, the Flight Attendant said, "Ladies and Gentlemen, welcome to Amarillo. Please remain in your seats with your seat belts fastened while the Captain taxis what's left of our airplane to the gate!"

- Another flight attendant's comment on a less than perfect landing: "We ask you to please remain seated as Captain Kangaroo bounces us to the terminal."

- A Canadian airline pilot wrote in his journal, a few years ago, that on one particular flight due to strong crosswinds, he had unfortunately hammered his ship onto the runway with a very hard greeting. The airline had a policy, which required the first officer on the flight to stand at the exit door while the passengers disembarked, to smile and repeat, "Thanks for flying our airline." His comments indicated that, in light of the poor landing, he avoided eye contact with the passengers in an attempt to avoid any smart comments that might result. Finally there was only one little old lady left to exit the plane. Walking slowly up the aisle with a cane, she approached the awaiting first officer and said, "Sir, do you mind if I ask you a question?" "Why, no, Ma'am," said the pilot. "What is it? "Did we land, or were we shot down?"

- After a real crusher of a landing in Phoenix, the Flight Attendant came on with, "Ladies and Gentlemen, please remain in your seats until Capt. Crash and the Crew have brought the aircraft to a screeching halt against the gate. And, once the tire smoke has cleared and the warning belts are silenced, we'll open the door and you can pick your way through the wreckage to the terminal."

- A plane was taking off from Kennedy Airport. After reaching a comfortable cruising altitude. The captain made an announcement over the intercom, "Ladies and Gentlemen. This is your captain speaking. Welcome to flight Number 293, nonstop from New York to Los Angeles. The weather ahead is good and, therefore, we should have a smooth and uneventful flight. Now sit back and relax. OH, MY GOD!" Silence followed, and after a few minutes, the captain came back on the intercom and said, "Ladies and Gentlemen, I am so sorry if I scared you earlier. While I was talking to you, the flight attendant brought me a cup of very hot coffee, which ended up spilling in my lap. You should see the front of my pants! A passenger in Coach yelled, "That's nothing. You should see the back of mine! (☺)

A WOMAN'S RANDOM THOUGHTS (☺)

1. Skinny people tick me off! Especially when they say things like, "You know sometimes I forget to eat." Now I've forgotten my address, my mother's maiden name, and even my keys. But I've never forgotten to eat. You have to be a special kind of stupid to forget to eat.

2. A friend of mine confused her valium with her birth control pills. She had 12 kids, but she doesn't give a s**t.

3. They keep telling us to get in touch with our bodies. Mine isn't all that communicative but I heard from it the other day after I said, "Body, how'd you like to go to the nine o'clock class in vigorous toning?" Clear as a bell my body said, "Listen B***h do it & you die." The trouble with some women is that they get all excited about nothing (and then they marry him.)

4. I read this article that said the typical symptoms of stress are eating too much, smoking too much, impulse buying and driving too fast. Are they kidding? That is my idea of a perfect day.

5. I know what victoria's Secret is. The secret is that nobody older than 20 can fit into their stuff.

6. If men can run the world, why can't they stop wearing neckties? How intelligent is it to start the day by tying a noose around your neck?

(☺) (☺) (☺)

I WANNA TAKE IT BACK ☹

Have you ever spoken and wished that you could immediately take the words back or that you could crawl into a hole? Here are the testimonials of a few people who did.

1. I walked into a hair salon with my husband and three kids in tow and asked loudly, "How much do you charge for a shampoo and a blow job?" I turned around and walked back out and never went back. My husband didn't say a word. He knew better.

2. I was at the golf store comparing different kinds of golf balls. I was unhappy with the women's type I had been using. After browsing for several minutes, I was approached by one of the good looking gentlemen who work at the store. He asked if he could help me. Without thinking, I looked at him and said, "I think I like playing with men's balls."

3. My sister and I were at the mall and passed by a store that sold a variety of candy and nuts. As we were looking at the display case, the boy behind the counter asked if we needed any help. I replied, "No, I'm just looking at your nuts." My sister started to laugh hysterically, the boy grinned, and I turned beet red and walked away. To this day, my sister has never let me forget.

4. Have you ever asked your child a question too many times? My three-year old son had a lot of problems with potty training

and I was on him constantly. One day we stopped at Taco Bell for a quick lunch in between errands it was very busy, with a full dining room. While enjoying my taco, I smelled something funny, so of course I checked my seven month old daughter, and she was clean. Then I realized that Danny had not asked to go potty in a while, so I asked him if he needed to go, and he said, "No." I kept thinking, "Oh lord, that child has had an accident, and I don't have any clothes with me." Then I said, "Danny, are you SURE you didn't have an accident?" "No," he replied I just knew that he must have had an accident, because the smell was getting worse. So, I asked one more time, "Danny, did you have an accident?" This time he jumped up, yanked down his pants, bent over and spread his cheeks and yelled. "SEE MOM, IT's JUST FARTS!"
While 30 people nearly choked to death on their tacos laughing, he calmly pulled up his pants and sat down. An old couple made me feel better by thanking me for the best laugh they'd ever had!

5. This had most of the state of Michigan laughing for 2 days and a very embarrassed female news anchor! Who will, in the future, likely think before she speaks. What happens when you predict snow but don't get any? A true story. We had a female news anchor that the day after it was supposed to have snowed and didn't turned to the weatherman and asked: "So Bob, where's that 8 inches you promised me last night?" Not only did he have to leave the set, but half the crew did too!

NAVAJO MESSAGE FOR THE MOON

When NASA was preparing for the Apollo Project, it took the astronauts to a Navajo reservation in Arizona for training. One day, a Navajo elder and his son came across the space crew walking among the rocks. The elder, who spoke only Navajo, asked a question. His son translated for the NASA people: "What are these guys in the big suits doing?"

One of the astronauts said that they were practicing for a trip to the moon. When his son relayed this comment the Navajo elder got all excited and asked if it would be possible to give to the astronauts a message to deliver to the moon.

Recognizing a promotional opportunity when he saw one, a NASA official accompanying the astronauts said, "Why certainly!" and told an underling to get a tape recorder. The Navajo elder's comments into the microphone were brief. The NASA official asked the son if he would translate what his father had said. The son listened to the recording and laughed uproariously. But he refused to translate.

So the NASA people took the tape to a nearby Navajo village and played it for other members of the tribe. They too laughed long and loudly but also refused to translate the elder's message to the moon.

An official government translator was summoned. After he finally stopped laughing the translator relayed the message: "WATCH OUT FOR THESE ASSHOLES. THEY HAVE COME TO STEAL YOUR LAND." (☺)

HAPPY THANKSGIVING

A young man named John received a parrot as a gift. The parrot had a bad attitude and an even worse vocabulary. Every word out of the bird's mouth was rude, obnoxious and laced with profanity.

John tried and tried to change the bird's attitude by consistently saying only polite words, playing soft music and anything else he could think of to "clean up" the bird's vocabulary. Finally, John was fed up and he yelled at the parrot. The parrot yelled back. John shook the parrot and the parrot got angrier and even ruder. In desperation, John threw up his hands, grabbed the bird and put him in the freezer. For a few minutes the parrot squawked and kicked and screamed. Then suddenly there was total quiet. Not a peep was heard for over a minute. Fearing that he'd hurt the parrot, John quickly opened the door to the freezer. The parrot calmly stepped out onto John's outstretched arms and said, "I believe I may have offended you with my rude language and actions. I'm sincerely remorseful for my inappropriate transgressions and I fully intend to do everything I can to correct my rude and unforgivable behavior."

John was stunned at the change in the bird's attitude. He was about to ask the parrot what had made such a dramatic change in his behavior, when the bird continued, "May I ask what the turkey did?" (☺)

THE AMERICAN SOLDIER

Took place in London.

The train was very crowded, so the American soldier walked the length of the train, looking for an empty seat. The only unoccupied seat was directly adjacent to a well-dressed middle aged French lady and was being used by her little dog. The war weary soldier asked, "Please ma'am, may I sit in that seat?" The French woman looked down her nose at the soldier, sniffed and said, "You Americans. You are such a rude class of people. Can't you see my little Fiji is using that seat?" The soldier walked away, determined to find a place to rest, but after another trip down to the end of the train, found himself again facing the woman with the dog. Again, he asked, "Please lady, may I sit there? I'm very tired." The French woman wrinkled her nose and snorted, "You Americans! Not only are you rude, you are also arrogant."

The soldier didn't say anything else: he leaned over, picked up the little dog, tossed it out the window of the train and sat down in the empty seat. The woman shrieked and railed, and demanded that someone defend her honor and chastise the soldier.

An English gentleman sitting across the aisle spoke up. "You know, sir, you Americans do seem to have a penchant for doing the wrong things. You eat holding the fork in the wrong hand. You drive your cars on the wrong side of the road. And now, sir, you've thrown the wrong bitch out the window." (☺)

FLY A KITE (☺)

This guy in his back yard is trying to fly a kite. He throws the kite up in the air, the wind catches it for a few seconds, then comes crashing back down to earth. He tries this a few more times with no success.
All the while, his wife is watching from the kitchen window. Muttering to herself how men need to be told how to do everything. She opens the window and yells to her husband. "You need a piece of tail."
The man turns with a confused look on his face and yells back. "Make up your mind last night you told me to go fly a kite." ☹

BUBBA'S PSYCHIATRIST

Bubba went to a psychiatrist. "I've got problems. Every time I go to bed, I think there's somebody under it. I'm scared. I think I'm going crazy."

"Put yourself in my hands for one year said the shrink. "Come talk to me three times a week, and we should be able to get rid of those fears."

"How much do you charge?"

"Eighty dollars per visit" Replied the doctor.

"I'll sleep on it," said Bubba.

Six months later the doctor met Bubba on the street. "Why didn't you ever come to see me about those fears you were having?" asked the psychiatrist.

"Well, eighty bucks a visit three times a week for a year is an awful lot of money! A bartender cured me for $10. I was so happy to have saved all that money I went and bought me a new pickup!"

"Is that so? And how, may I ask, did a bartender cure you?"

"He told me to cut the legs off the bed! Ain't nobody under there now!"

NOAH IN THE YEAR 2012

In the year 2011, the Lord came unto Noah, who was now living in the United States, and said, "Once again, the earth has become wicked and over-populated, and I see the end of a flood before me. Build another Ark and save 2 of every living thing along with a few good humans.
He gave Noah the blueprints, saying, "You have 6 months to build the Ark before I will start the un-ending rain for 40 days and 40 nights."

Six months later, the Lord looked down and saw Noah weeping in his yard but no Ark. "Noah!" He roared, "I'm about to start the rain! Where is the Ark?"

"Forgive me, Lord, "begged Noah, "but things have changed. I needed a building permit. I've been arguing with the inspector about the need for a sprinkler system. My neighbors claim that I've violated the neighborhood zoning laws by building the Ark in my yard and exceeding the height limitations. We had to go to the development Appeal Board for a decision.

Then the Department of Transportation demanded a bond be posted for the future cost of moving power lines and other overhead obstructions, to clear the passage for the Ark's move to the sea. I told them that the sea would be coming to us, but they would hear nothing of it.

Getting the wood was another problem. There's a ban on cutting local trees in order to save the spotted owl. I tried to convince the environmentalists that I needed the wood to save the owls- but no go!

When I started gathering the animals, an animal rights group sued me. They insisted that I was confining wild animals against their will.

They argued the accommodations were too restrictive, and it was cruel and inhumane to put so many animals in a confined space.

Then the EPA ruled that I couldn't build the Ark until they'd conducted an environmental impact study on your proposed flood.

I'm still trying to resolve a complaint with the Human Rights Commission on how many minorities I'm supposed to hire for my building crew. Immigration and Naturalization is checking the green-card status of most of the people who want to work.

The trades unions say I can't use my sons. They insist I have to hire only Union workers with Ark-building experience.

To make matters worse, the IRS seized all my assets, claiming I'm trying to leave the country illegally with endangered species.

So, "forgive! me, Lord, but it would take at least 10 years for me to finish this Ark."

Suddenly the skies cleared, the sun began to shine, and a rainbow stretched across the sky. Noah looked up in wonder and asked, "You mean you're not going to destroy the world?"

"No," said the Lord. "The government beat me to it."

Note: So True ☹

THE GUINNESS BOOK

Sleeping Beauty, Tom Thumb, and Quasimodo were all talking one day. Sleeping Beauty said, "I believe myself to be the most beautiful girl in the world."
Tom Thumb said. "I must be the smallest person in the world."
Quasimodo said "I absolutely have to be the ugliest and most obnoxious person in the world."

So they all decided to go to the Guinness Book of World Records to have their claims verified.

1. Sleeping Beauty went in first and came out looking deliriously happy. "It's official; I AM the most beautiful girl in the world."
2. Tom Thumb went next and emerged triumphant, "I AM now officially the smallest person in the world."
3. Sometime later Quasimodo comes out looking utterly confused and says, "Who the hell is Rosie O'Donnell?

JUST TAKE THE MONEY (☺)

Jack, a handsome man, walked into a sports bar around 9:58 pm. He sat down next to this blonde at the bar and stared up at the TV. The 10:00 news was on.

The news crew was covering a story of a man on a ledge of a large building preparing to jump.

The blonde looked at jack and said, "Do you think he'll jump?" Jack says, "You know, I bet he will."

The blonde replied, "Well, I bet he won't."

Jack place $30 on the bar and said, "You're on!"

Just as the blonde placed her money on the bar, the guy did a swan dive off of the building, falling to his death.

The blonde was very upset and handed her $30.00 to Jack, saying, "Fair's fair. Here's your money."

Jack replied, "I can't take your money, I saw this earlier on the 5 o'clock news and knew he would jump."

The blonde replies, "I did too; but I didn't think he'd do it again."

Jack took the money.

BULL (☺)

American touring Spain stopped at a local restaurant following a day of sightseeing. While slipping his sangria, he noticed a sizzling, scrumptious looking platter being served at the next table. Not only did it look good, the smell was wonderful. He asked the waiter, "What is that you just served?" The waiter replied, "Ah senor, you have excellent taste! Those are bull's testicles from the bull fight this morning. A delicacy!"

The American, though momentarily daunted, said, "What the hell, I'm on vacation! Bring me an order!" The waiter replied, "I am so sorry senor. There is only one serving per day because there is only one bull fight each morning. If you come early tomorrow and place your order, we will be sure to save you this delicacy!"

The next morning, the American returned, placed his order, and then that evening he was served the one and only special delicacy of the day. After a few bites, and inspecting the contents of his platter, he called to the waiter and said, "These are delicious, but they are much, much smaller than the ones I saw you serve yesterday!"

The waiter shrugged his shoulders and replied, "Si senor. Sometimes the bull wins." ☹

BS

A pheasant was standing in a field chatting to a bull. "I would love to be able to get to the top of yonder tree", the pheasant said with a sigh, "but I haven't got the energy". "Well, why don't you nibble on some of my droppings?" replied the bull. "They're packed with nutrients". The pheasant pecked at a lump of dung and found that it actually gave him enough strength to reach the first branch of the tree. The next day, after some more dung, he reached the second branch. And so on. Finally, after a fortnight, there he was proudly perched at the top of the tree. Whereupon he was spotted by a farmer who dashed into the farmhouse, emerged with a shotgun, and shot the peasant right out of the tree.

Moral of the story: Bull s**t might get you to the top, but it won't keep you there.

MIRACLE OF TOILET PAPER (☺ ☹)

Fresh from my shower, I stand in front of the mirror complaining to my husband that my breasts are too small. Instead of characteristically telling me it's not so, he uncharacteristically comes up with a suggestion. "If you want your breasts to grow, then every day take a piece of Toilet paper and rub it between your breasts for a few seconds." Willing to try anything, I fetch a piece of toilet paper and stand in front of the mirror, rubbing it between my breasts. "How long will this take?" I asked. "They will grow larger over a period of years," my husband replies. I stopped. "Do you really think rubbing a piece of toilet paper between my breasts every day will make my breasts larger over the years?" Without missing a beat he says "Worked for your butt, didn't it?"

He's still alive and with a great deal of therapy, may even walk again. Stupid, stupid man. (☺ ☹)

HOW TO MAKE A WOMAN HAPPY – VS. – HOW TO MAKE A MAN HAPPY.

How to make a woman happy.

A man only needs to be:

- A friend
- A companion
- A lover
- An electrician
- A carpenter
- A plumber
- A mechanic
- A pest exterminator
- A good listener
- An organizer
- A good father
- Very clean
- Sympathetic
- Athletic
- Warm
- Attentive
- Gallant
- Intelligent
- Funny
- Creative

- Tender
- Strong
- Understanding
- Tolerant
- Prudent
- Ambitious
- Capable
- Courageous
- Determined
- True
- Dependable
- Passionate
- Compassionate
- Give her compliments regularly
- Give her lots of attention, but expect little yourself
- Never and I mean never forget – Birthdays, Anniversaries, and all Arrangements she makes for you.

How to make a man happy.

- Never have a headache
- Show up naked
- Bring food
- Hand over the remote (☺) That's it

ACTUAL AUSTRALIAN COURT DOCKET 12659 – CASE OF THE PREGNANT LADY.

A lady about 8 months pregnant got on a bus. She noticed the man opposite her was smiling at her. She immediately moved to another seat. This time the smile turned into a grin, so she moved again. The man seemed more amused.

When on the fourth move, the man burst out laughing, she complained to the driver and he had the man arrested.

The case came up in court. The judge asked the man (about 20 years old) what he had to say for himself. The man replied, "Well your Honor, it was like this:

A...When the lady got on the bus, I couldn't help but notice her condition. She sat under a sweets sign that said, "The double Mint Twins are coming" and I grinned.

B...Then she moved and sat under a sign that said, "Logan's Liniment will reduce the swelling", and I had to smile.

C...Then she placed herself under a deodorant sign that said, "Williams's Big Stick Did the Trick", and I could hardly contain myself.

D...But, your Honor, when she moved the fourth time and sat under a sign that said, "Goodyear rubber could have prevented this Accident." I just lost it."

"CASE DISMISSED!"

A VIEW INTO THE NOT SO DISTANT FUTURE - OR IS IT NOW? (☺ ☹)

Operator	:	"Thank you for calling Pizza Hut, May I have your…"
Customer	:	"Hi, I'd like to order."
Operator	:	"May I have your NIDN first, sir?"
Customer	:	"My National ID Number, yeah, hold on, It's 6102049998-45-54610."
Operator	:	"Thank you, Mr. Sheehan. I see you live at 1742 Meadowland Drive, and the phone # 494-2366. Your office # over at Lincoln Insurance is 745-2302 and your cell # 266-2566. You are calling from you're cell phone. Where should your order be delivered?
Customer	:	"Huh? To my home. Where d'ya get all this information?"
Operator	:	"We're wired into the system, sir."
Customer	:	(Sighs) "Oh, well, I'd like to order a couple of your All-Meat special pizzas."
Operator	:	"I don't think that's a good idea, sir."
Customer	:	"What do you mean?"
Operator	:	"Sir, your medical records indicate that you've got very high blood pressure and extremely high cholesterol. Your national Health Care provider won't allow such an unhealthy choice."
Customer	:	"What do you recommend, then?"
Operator	:	"You might try our low-fat soybean Yogurt Pizza. I'm sure you'll like it."

Customer	:	"What makes you think I'd like something like that?
Operator	:	"Well, you checked out "Gourmet soybean Recipes" from your local library last week, sir. That's why I made the suggestion."
Customer	:	"All right, all right, Give me two family-sized ones, then.What's the damage?"
Operator	:	"That should be plenty for you, your wife and four kids, sir. The "damage," as you put it, comes to $49.99."
Customer	:	"Let me give you my credit card number."
Operator	:	"I'm sorry sir, but I'm afraid you'll have to pay in cash. Your credit card balance is over its limit."
Customer	:	"I'll run over to the ATM and get some cash before you're driver gets here."
Operator	:	"That won't work either, sir. Your checking account only shows $5 available and I do not see any other accounts listed for you or you're wife."
Customer	:	"Never mind. Just send the pizzas. I'll have the cash ready. How long will it take?"
Operator	:	"We're running a little behind, sir. It'll be about 45 minutes, Sir. If you're in a hurry you might want to pick'em up while you're out getting the cash, but carrying pizzas on a motorcycle can be a little awkward."
Customer	:	"How do you know I'm riding a bike?"
Operator	:	"It says here you're in default on your car payments, so your car got repo'ed. But your Harley's paid up, so I just assumed that you'd be using it."
Customer	:	@#%#*%
Operator	:	"I'd advise watching your language, sir. You've already got a July 2010 conviction for cussing out a cop.."
Customer	:	(Speechless)
Operator	:	"Will there be anything else, sir?"
Customer	:	"No, nothing. Oh, yeah, don't forget the two free liters of Coke your ad says I get with the pizzas."
Operator	:	"I'm sorry sir, but our ad's exclusionary clause prevents us from offering free soda to diabetics."

☺ **And who says government isn't great** ☹

TEACHING MATH ☹

Last week I purchased a burger at Burger King for $1.58. The counter girl took my $2 and I was digging for my change when I pulled 8 cents from my pocket and gave it to her. She stood there, holding the nickel and 3 pennies, while looking at the screen on her register.

I sensed her discomfort and tried to tell her to just give me two quarters, but she hailed the manager for help.

While he tried to explain the transaction to her, she stood there and cried.

Why do I tell you this?

Because of the evolution in teaching math since the 1950's

- Teaching math in 1950 – A logger sells a truckload of lumber for $100. His cost of production is 4/5 of the price. What is his profit?
- Teaching Math in 1960 – A logger sells a truckload of lumber for $100. His cost of production is 4/5 of the price, or $80. What is his profit?
- Teaching Math in 1970 – A logger sells a truckload of lumber for $100. His cost of production is $80. Did he make a profit?
- Teaching Math in 1980 – A logger sells a truckload of lumber for $100. His cost of production is $80 and his profit is $20. Your assignment: Underline the number 20.
- Teaching Math in 1990 – A logger cuts down a beautiful forest because he is selfish and inconsiderate and cares nothing for the habitat of animals or the preservation of our woodlands. He does this so he can make a profit of $20. What do you think of

this way of making a living? Topic for class participation after answering the question: How the birds and squirrels felt as the logger cut down their homes? (There are no wrong answers.)

- <u>Teaching Math in 2005</u> – El hachero vende un camion carga por $100. La cuesta de production es…

THOUGHTS TO PONDER
ON A RAINY DAY (☺)

1. Does a clean house indicate that there is a broken computer in it?
2. Why is it that no matter what color of bubble bath you use the bubbles are always white?
3. Is there ever a day that mattresses are not on sale?
4. Why do people constantly return to the refrigerator with hopes that something new to eat will have materialized?
5. On electric toasters, why do they engrave the message "one slice"? How many pieces of bread do they think people are really going to try to stuff in that slot?
6. Why do people keep running over a string a dozen times with their vacuum cleaner, then reach down, pick it up, examine it, then put it down to give the vacuum one more chance?
7. Why is it that no plastic garbage bag will open from the end you first try?
8. How do those dead bugs get into those closed light fixtures?
9. Considering all the lint you get in your dryer, if you kept drying your clothes would they eventually just disappear?
10. When we are in the supermarket and someone rams our ankle with a shopping cart than apologizes for doing so, why do we say, "It's all right?" Well, it isn't all right so why don't we say, "That hurt, you stupid idiom?"
11. Why is it that whenever you attempt to catch something that's falling off the table you always manage to knock something else over?

12. Is it true that the only difference between a year sale and a trash pickup is how close to the road the stuff is placed

13. In winter why do we try to keep the house as warm as it was in summer when we complained about the heat?

14. How come we never hear father-in-law jokes?

15. If at first you don't succeed, shouldn't you try doing it like your wife told you do it?

16. The statistics on sanity are that one out of every four persons is suffering from some sort of mental illness. Now think of your three best friends, if they're okay, then it's? (☺)

MAN'S RULES FOR WOMEN

Please note: These are all numbered "1" ON PURPOSE! (☺)

1. Learn to work the toilet seat. You're a big girl. If it's up, put it down. We need it up, you need it down. You don't hear us complaining about you leaving it down.
1. Sunday sports, it's like the full moon or the changing of the tides. Let it be.
1. Shopping is NOT a sport. And no, we are never going to think of it that way.
1. Crying is blackmail.
1. Ask for what you want. Let us be clear on this one: Subtle hints do not work! Strong hints do not work! Obviously hints do not work! Just say it!
1. Yes and No are perfectly acceptable answers to almost every question.
1. Come to us with a problem only if you want help solving it. That's what we do. Sympathy is what girlfriends are for.
1. A headache that lasts for 17 months is a problem. See a doctor.
1. Anything we said 6 months ago is inadmissible in an argument. In fact, all comments become null and void after 7 days.
1. If you won't dress like the Victoria's Secret girls, don't expect us to act like soap opera guys.
1. If you think you're fat in that outfit. Don't ask us.
1. If something we said can be interpreted two ways and one of the ways makes you sad or angry, we meant the other one.

1. You can either ask us to do something or tell us how you want it done. Not both. If you already know best how to do it, then just do it yourself.
1. Whenever possible, please say whatever you have to say during commercials.
1. Christopher Columbus did not need directions and neither do we.
1. All men see in only 16 colors, Like Windows default settings. Peach, for example, is a fruit, not a color. Pumpkin is also a fruit. We have no idea what Mauve is.
1. If it itches, it will be scratched. We do that.
1. If we ask what is wrong and you say "nothing," we will act like nothing's wrong. We know you are lying, but it is just not worth the hassle.
1. If you ask a question you don't want an answer to, expect an answer you don't want to hear.
1. When we have to go somewhere, absolutely anything you wear is fine…Really.
1. Don't ask us what we're thinking about unless you are prepared to discuss such topics as, baseball, the shotgun formation, or monster trucks.
1. You have enough clothes.
1. You have too many shoes.
1. I am in shape. Round is a shape.
1. Thank you for reading Men's Rules: And yes I know I have to sleep on the couch tonight, but did you know men really don't mind that, it's like camping.

MOTHERS ADVISE TO HER DAUGHTER (☺)

1. Don't imagine you can change a man unless he's in diapers.
2. What do you do if your boyfriend walks out the door? You shut the door.
3. If they put a man on the moon, they should be able to put them all up there.
4. Never let your man's mind wander, its to little to be out alone.
5. Go for younger men. You might as well, they never mature anyway.
6. Men are all the same, they just have different faces, so that we can tell them apart.
7. Definition of a bachelor; a man who has missed the opportunity to make some women miserable.
8. Women don't make fools of men; most of them are the do-it-yourself types.
9. The best way to get a man to do something is to suggest they are to old for it.
10. Love is blind, but marriage is a real eye-opener.
11. If you want a committed man, look in a mental hospital.
12. The children of Israel wandered around the desert for 40 years. Even in biblical times, men wouldn't ask for directions.
13. If he asks what sort of books you're interested in, tell him checkbooks.
14. Remember a sense of humor does not mean that you tell him jokes; it means that you laugh at his.

THE TELEPHONE

South Carolina farm wife called the local phone company to report her telephone failed to ring when her friends called – and that on the few occasions when it did ring, her dog always moaned right before the phone rang.

The telephone repairman proceeded to the scene, curious to see this psychic dog or senile lady.

Upon arriving at the residence he climbed the utility pole, plugged in his test set, and dialed the subscriber's phone number.

The phone didn't ring right away, but then the dog moaned and then the telephone began to ring.

Climbing down from the pole, the telephone repairman discovered the following:

1. The dog was tied to the telephone system's ground wire with a steel chain and collar.
2. The wire connection to the ground rod was loose.
3. The dog was receiving 90 volts of signaling current when the number was called.
4. After a couple of jolts, the dog would start moaning and then urinate.

5. The wet ground would complete the circuit, thus causing the phone to ring.

<u>There is a moral</u>: Some problems can be fixed by pissing and moaning.

WOMEN?

Two women in heaven:

1st woman: Hi! My name is Wanda

2nd woman: Hi! I'm Sylvia. How'd you die?

1st woman: I Froze to Death.

2nd woman: How Horrible!

1st woman: It wasn't so bad. After I quit shaking from the cold, I began to get warm & sleepy, and finally died a peaceful death. What about you?

2nd woman: I died of a massive heart attack. I suspected that my husband was cheating, so I came home early to catch him, but instead, I found him all by himself in the den watching TV.

1st woman: So, what happened?

2nd woman: I was so sure there was another woman there somewhere that I started running all over the house looking. I ran up into the attic and searched, and down into the basement. Then I went through every closet and checked under all the beds. I kept this up until I had looked everywhere, and finally I became so exhausted that I just keeled over with a heart attack and died.

1st woman: Too bad you didn't look in the freezer; we'd both still be alive

NO CHILD LEFT BEHIND – IN MASSACHUSETTS

Reaching to Federal Guidelines, the state of Massachusetts, which has been highlighted as a role model for student testing by two U.S. Senators from this State, released the following memo:

In response to the Federal No Child Left behind Act, students will have to pass it to be promoted to the next grade level. In the hopes that it will be uniformly adopted by all the states, thus illuminating Massachusetts to a glorious front runner position in education, it will be called: the **Federal Arithmetic and Reading Test** (FART).All students who cannot pass a FART in the second grade will be retested in grades 3-5 until such a time as they are capable of achieving a FART score of 80%. If a student does not successfully FART by grade 5, that student shall be placed in a separate English program, the **Special Massachusetts Elective for Learning Language** (SMELL). The student can graduate to middle school by taking a one-semester course in **Comprehensive Reading and Arithmetic Preparation** (CRAP). If by age fourteen the student cannot FART, SMELL, or CRAP, he or she will earn a promotion in an intensive one-week seminar. This is the **Preparatory Reading for Unprepared Nationally Exempted Students** (PRUNES). It is the opinion of the Massachusetts Department of Public Instruction that an intensive week of PRUNES will enable any student to FART, SMELL or CRAP.

U.S. Senators Ted Kennedy and John Kerry stated that this revised provision of the student-testing program should help clear the air.

12 ZINGERS FOR THE LADIES

1. One day my housework-challenged husband decided to wash his Sweat shirt. Seconds after he stepped into the laundry room, he shouted to me, "What setting do I use on the washing machine?" "It depends," I replied. "What does it say on your shirt?" He yelled back. "University of Oklahoma."

2. A couple is lying in bed. The man says, "I am going to make you the happiest woman in the world." The woman replies, "I'll Miss you…"

3. "It's just too hot to wear clothes today,' Jack says as he stepped out of the shower, "honey, what do you think the neighbors would think if I mowed the lawn like this?" "Probably that I married you for your Money," she replied.

4. He said – Shall we try swapping positions tonight? She said – That's a good idea…you stand by the ironing board while I sit on the sofa and Fart.

5. Q : What do you call an intelligent good looking, sensitive man?
    A : A rumor

6. A man and his wife, now in their 60's were celebrating their 40th wedding anniversary. On their special day a good fairy came to them and said that because they had been so good that each one of them could have one wish. The wife wished for a trip around the

world with her husband. Whoosh! Immediately she had airline/cruise tickets in her hands. The man wished for a female companion 30 years younger…Whoosh…immediately he turned ninety!!! Gotta love that fairy! ()

7. Dear Lord. I pray for <u>Wisdom</u> to understand my man; <u>Love</u> to forgive him. And <u>Patience</u> for his moods. Because, Lord, if I pray for <u>Strength,</u> I'll beat him to death. AMEN.

8. Q : Why do little boys whine?
    A : They are practicing to be men.

9. Q : What do you call a handcuffed man?
    A : Trustworthy.

10. Q : What does it mean when a man is in your bed gasping for breath and calling your name?
    A : You did not hold the pillow down long enough.

11. Q : Why do men whistle when they are sitting on the toilet?
    A : It helps them remember which end they need to wipe.

12. Q : How do you keep your husband from reading your e-mail?
    A : Rename the mail folder "instruction Manuals"

Note: We still love you guys. (☺)

WHAT ARE SENIORS
WORTH ANYWAY?

Remember old folks are worth a fortune, with silver in their hair, gold in their teeth, stones in their kidneys, lead in their feet, and gas in their stomachs.

Dear sister Amanda

I have become a little older since I saw you last and a few changes have come into my life since then. Frankly, I have become quite a frivolous old gal. I am seeing four gentlemen every day. I visit the John several times a day, what a gas. Then Charlie Horse comes along, and when he is here, he takes a lot of my time and attention. When he leaves, Arthur Ritis shows up and stays the rest of the day. He doesn't like to stay in one place very long, so he takes me from joint to joint. After such a busy day I'm really tired and glad to get to bed with Ben Gay. What a life!

P.S. The preacher came to call the other day. He said at my age I should be thinking about the hereafter. I told him, "Oh, I do all the time. No matter where I am, in the parlor, upstairs, in the kitchen or down in the basement, I ask myself, what am I here after.
Love big sister Jennifer.

18 SURE FIRE WAYS YOU CAN TELL WHEN IT'S GOING TO BE A ROTTEN DAY ☹

- You wake up face down on the pavement.
- You put your bra on backwards and it fits better.
- You call Suicide Prevention and they put you on hold.
- You see a "60 Minutes" news team waiting in your office.
- Your birthday cake collapses from the weight of the candles.
- You want to put on the clothes you wore home from the party and there aren't any.
- You turn on the news and they're showing emergency routes out of the city.
- Your twin sister forgot your birthday.
- You wake up and discover your waterbed broke and then realize that you don't have a waterbed.
- Your car horn goes off accidentally and remains stuck as you follow a group of hell's Angels on the freeway.
- Your boss tells you not to bother to take off your coat.
- The bird singing outside your window is a buzzard.
- You wake up and your braces are locked together.
- You walk to work and find your dress is stuck in the back of your pantyhose.
- You call your answering service and they tell you it's none of your business.
- Your blind date turns out to be your ex.
- Your income tax check bounces.
- You put both contact lenses in the same eye.

TWO OLD MEN SWAPPING THOUGHTS FOR THE DAY

1ˢᵗ Old man: Give a person a fish and you feed them for a day; teach that person to use the internet and they won't bother you for weeks.

2ⁿᵈ Old man: Some people are like Slinkies...not really good for anything, but you still can't help but smile when you see one tumble down the stairs.

1ˢᵗ Old man: Health nuts are going to feel stupid someday, lying in hospitals dying of nothing.

2ⁿᵈ Old man: Have you noticed since everyone has a camcorder these days no one talks about seeing UFOs like they use to.

1ˢᵗ Old man: According to a recent survey, men say the first thing they notice about women are their eyes, and women say the first thing they notice about men is they're a bunch of liars.

2ⁿᵈ Old man: Whenever I feel blue, I start breathing again.

1ˢᵗ Old man: All of us could take a lesson from the weather. It pays no attentions to criticism.

2ⁿᵈ Old man: Why does a slight tax increase cost you two hundred dollars and a substantial tax cut saves you thirty cents?

1ˢᵗ Old man: In the 60's people took acid to make the world weird. Now the world is weird and people take Prozac to make it normal.

2ⁿᵈ Old man: Politics is supposed to be the second oldest profession. I have come to realize that it bears a very close resemblance to the first.

1ˢᵗ Old man: How is it one careless match can start a forest fire, but it takes a whole box to start a campfire?

2ⁿᵈ Old man: You read about all these terrorist – most of them came here legally, but they hung around on these expired visas, some for as long as 10-15 years. Now, compare that to Blockbuster; you are two days late with a video and those people are all over you. Let's put Blockbuster in charge of immigration.

1ˢᵗ Old man: "All I ask is a chance to prove that money can't make me happy."

2ⁿᵈ Old man: "I know God won't give me anything I can't handle. I just wish he didn't trust me so much."

1ˢᵗ Old man: I got to go take my meds now see ya tomorrow.

2ⁿᵈ Old man: Hell I am late for my meds. See ya later.

A MAN HAS NEEDS

I've never quite figured out why the sexual urges of men & women differ so much. I never have figured out the whole Venus and Mars thing. I have never figured out why men think with their head and women with their heart. I have never figured out why the sexual desire gene gets thrown into a state of turmoil when it hears the words "I do."

One evening last week, my wife and I were getting into bed. Well, the passion starts to heat up and she eventually says, "I don't feel like it, I just want you to hold me." I said "What?" So she says the words that every husband on the planet dreads to hear…"You must not be in tune with my emotional needs as a woman." I am thinking, "What was her first clue?" I finally realize that nothing was going to happen that night so I went to sleep.

The very next day, we went shopping at a big unnamed department store. I walked around with her while she tried on three different very expensive outfits. She couldn't decide which one to take so I told her to take all three. She wanted matching shoes. So I said, "Let's get a pair for each outfit." We went to the jewelry department where she gets a pair of diamond earrings. Let me tell you, she was so excited. She must have thought I was one wave short of a shipwreck. I started to think she was testing me because she asked for a tennis bracelet when she doesn't even know how to play tennis. I think I threw her for a loop when I said it was okay. She was almost sexually excited from all of this. You should have seen her face when she said, "I think this is all dear, let's go to the cash register."

I could hardly contain myself when I blurted out, "No honey, I don't feel like buying all of this stuff now." You should have seen her face…it went completely blank. I then said, "Really honey! I just want you to HOLD this stuff for a while." And just when she had this look like she was going to kill me! I added, "You must not be in tune with my financial needs as a man." I figure that I won't be having sex again until sometime after the spring of 2014. (☺) (☹)

MARRIAGE

(For all you women out there, enjoy this. For all you guys out there...hope you can take a joke!)

Newlywed Rules.

Marriage (Part 1) Typical macho man married typical good-looking lady and after the wedding, he laid down the following rules:

"I'll be home when I want, if I want and at what time I want, and I don't expect any hassle from you. I expect a great dinner to be on the table unless I tell you that I won't be home for dinner. I'll go hunting, fishing, boozing and card-playing when I want with my old buddies and don't you give me a hard time about it. Those are my rules. Any comments?"

His new bride said. "No, that's fine with me. Just understand that there will be sex here at seven o'clock every night...whether you're here or not."

Damn she's good!

Marriage (Part 2) Husband and wife had a bitter quarrel on the day of their 40th wedding anniversary! The husband yells, "When you die, I'm getting you a headstone that reads, "Here Lies My Wife – Cold As Ever."

"Yeah?" she replies. "When you die, I'm getting you a headstone that reads, "Here Lies My Husband Stiff at last." (Ouch!)

He Asked for It!

Marriage (Part 3) Husband (a doctor) and his wife are having a fight at the breakfast table. Husband gets up in a rage and says, "And you are no good in bed either," and storms out of the house.

After sometimes he realizes he was nasty and decides to make amends and rings her up. She comes to the phone after many rings, and the irritated husband says, "what took you so long to answer the phone?" She says, "I was in bed." "In bed this early, doing what?" "Getting a second opinion!"

Yep, he had that coming, too!

Marriage (Part 4) A man has six children and is very proud of his achievement. He is so proud of himself, that he starts calling his wife, "Mother of Six" in spite of her objections.

One night, they go to a party. The man decides that it's time to go home and wants to find out if his wife is ready to leave as well. He shouts at the top of his voice, "Shall we go home Mother of six?"

His wife, irritated by her husband's lack of discretion shouts right back, "Anytime you're ready, Father of Four."

(☺) **Just a thought**: God may have created man before woman but there is always a rough draft before the masterpiece.

GOT TO LOVE THIS JUDGE!!!

In Florida, an atheist became incensed over the preparation for Easter and Passover holidays and decided to contact the local ACLU about the discrimination inflicted on atheists by the constant celebrations afforded to Christians and Jews with all their holidays while the atheists had no holiday to celebrate.

The ACLU jumped on the opportunity to once again pick up the cause of the godless and assigned their sharpest attorney's to the case. The case was brought before a wise judge who after listening to the long, passionate presentation of the ACLU lawyers promptly banged his gavel and declared, "Case dismissed!"

The lead ACLU lawyer immediately stood and objected to the ruling and said, "Your honor, how can you possibly dismiss this case? Surely the Christians have Christmas, Easter and many other observances. And the Jews, why in addition to Passover they have Yom Kippur and Hanukkah, and yet my client and all other atheists have no such holiday!"

The judge leaned forward in his chair and simply said "Obviously your client is too confused to know about or for that matter even celebrate the atheists' holiday!" The ACLU lawyer pompously said "We are aware of no such holiday for atheists, just what might that be, your honor?"

The judge said "Well it comes every year on exactly the same date...April 1st" "The fool says in his heart, "There is no God." Psalm 14:1, Psalm 53:1

Note :(You just got to love this judge) ☺

CHAPSTICK?

(A mother's memory)

So, we had this great 10 year old cat named Jack who just recently died. Jack was a great cat and the kids would carry him around and sit on him and nothing ever bothered him. He used to hang out and nap all day long on this mat in our bathroom.

Well we have 3 daughters and at the time of this story they Tootie who was 9 years old, and the twins Charlie and Natalie were 4 years old. The middle one Charlie, really loved chapstick. Just loved it. She kept asking to use my chapstick and then losing it. So finally one day I showed her where in the bathroom I keep my chapstick and how she could use it whenever she wanted to but she needed to put it back in the drawer when she was done.

Last year on Mother's Day, we were having the typical rush around and trying to get ready for Church with everyone crying and carrying on. My two twins are fighting over the toy in the cereal box. I am trying to fix the oldest daughter's hair and at the same time I am putting on my make-up. Everything is a mess and everyone has long forgotten that this is a wonderful day to honor me and the amazing job that is motherhood.

We finally have the oldest daughter Tootie and one twin Natalie, loaded in the car and I am looking for Charlie. I have searched everywhere and I finally round the corner to go into the bathroom. And there was Charlie. She was applying my chapstick very carefully to Jack's...rear end. Charlie looked right into my eyes and said "chapped."

Now if you have a cat, you know that she is right – their little butts do look pretty chapped. And, frankly, Jack didn't seem to mind.

The only question to really ask at that point was whether it was the first time Charlie had done that to the cats behind or the hundredth.

Note: Just remember no matter how hard you try to civilize these glorious little creatures, there will always be that day when you realize they've been using your chapstick on the cat's butt. ☺ ☹

FAMOUS PEOPLE SAY SOME OF THE DUMBEST THINGS

- **Question**: If you could live forever, would you and why? **Answer:** "I would not live forever, because we should not live forever, because if we were supposed to live forever, then we would live forever, but we cannot live forever, which is why I would not live forever." **Miss America 1995 from Alabama – <u>Heather Whitestone</u>**

- "Whenever I watch TV and see those poor starving kids all over the world, I can't help but cry. I mean I'd love to be skinny like that, but not with all those flies and death and stuff." **Popular -Pop singer – <u>Maria Carey</u>**

- "Smoking kills. If you're kissed, you've lost a very important part of your life," (**During an interview to become spokesperson for federal anti-smoking campaign.) <u>Brooke Shields</u>**

- "I've never had major knee surgery on any other part of my body." **University of Kentucky Basketball Forward – <u>Winston Bennett</u>**

- "Outside of the killings, Washington has one of the lowest crime rates in the country." **Washington DC Mayer – <u>Marion Barry</u>**

- "I'm not going to have some reporters pawing through our papers. We are the president." (Commenting on the release of subpoenaed documents.) **First Lady and Democratic Senator from New York – <u>Hillary Clinton</u>**

- "That lowdown scoundrel deserves to be kicked to death by a jackass, and I'm just the one to do it." **<u>A congressional candidate in Texas</u>**

- "Half this game is ninety percent mental." **Philadelphia Phillies Manager – <u>Danny Ozark</u>**
- "It isn't pollution that's harming the environment. It's the impurities in our air and water that are doing it." **Vice President – <u>Al Gore</u>**
- "We are ready for any unforeseen event that may or may not occur." **Vice President – <u>Al Gore</u>**
- "I love California. I practically grew up in Phoenix." Vice President – <u>Dan Quayle</u>
- "We've got to pause and ask ourselves, how much clean air do we need?" **Chrysler Chairman and CEO – <u>Lee Iacocca</u>**
- "The word "genius" isn't applicable in football. A genius is a guy like Norman Einstein." **NFL Quarterback and Sports Analyst – <u>Joe Theisman</u>**
- "We don't necessarily discriminate. We simply exclude certain types of people." **ROTC Instructor – <u>Colonel Gerald Wellman</u>**
- "If we don't succeed, we run the risk of failure." **President – <u>Bill Clinton</u>**
- "Traditionally, most of Australia's imports come from overseas." **<u>Keppel Elderberry</u>**
- "Your food stamps will be stopped effective March 1992 because we received notice that you passed away. May God bless you? You may reapply if there is a change in your circumstances." **Greenville, South Carolina – <u>Department of Social Services</u>**
- "If somebody has a bad heart, they can plug this jack in at night as they go to bed and it will monitor their heart throughout the night. And the next morning, when they wake up dead, there'll be a record." **FCC Chairman – <u>Mark S. Fowler</u>**

(☺☺☺☺) **Are we feeling any smarter.**

BY MY SIDE!

A woman's husband had been slipping in and out of a coma for several months, yet she had stayed by his bedside every single day. One day, he motioned for her to come nearer.

She sat by him, he whispered, eyes full of tears, "You know what? You have been with me all through the bad times.

When I got fired, you were there to support me.

When my business failed, you were there.

When I got shot, you were by my side.

When we lost the house, you stayed right here.

When my health started failing, you were still by my side...You know what?"

"What dear?" she gently asked, smiling as her heart began to fill with warmth.

"I think you're bad luck, get the %@#%@ away from me."

WHO SAID BLONDS ARE NOT SMART?

Three Blondes were all applying for the last available position on the Texas Highway Patrol. The detective conducting the interview looked at the three of them and said, "So y'all want to be cops, huh?" The blondes all nodded.

The detective got up, opened a file drawer and pulled out a folder. Sitting back down, he opened it and pulled out a picture, and said, "To be a police officer, you must be able to detect. You must be able to notice things such as distinguishing features and oddities such as scars and so forth."

So saying, he stuck the photo in the face of the first blonde and withdrew it after about two seconds. "Now," he said, "did you notice any distinguishing features about this man?"

The blonde immediately said, "Yes, I did. He has only one eye!"

The detective shook his head and said, "Of course he has only one eye in this picture! It's a profile of his face! You're dismissed!"

The first blonde hung her head and walked out of the office. The detective then turned to the second blonde, stuck the photo in her face for two seconds, pulled it back and said, "What about you? Notice anything unusual or outstanding about this man?"

"Yes! He only has one ear!"

The detective put his head in his hands and exclaimed, "Didn't you hear what I just told the other lady? This is a profile of the man's face! Of course you can only see one ear! You're excused too!"

The second blonde sheepishly walked out of the office.

The detective turned his attention to the third and last blonde and said, "This is probably a waste of time, but…"He flashed the photo in her face for a couple of seconds and withdrew it, saying, "All right, did you notice anything distinguishing or unusual about this man?"

The blonde said, "I sure did. This man wears contact lenses."

The detective frowned, took another look at the picture and began looking at some of the papers in the folder. He looked up at the blonde with a puzzled expression and said, "You're absolutely right! His bio says he wears contacts! How in the world could you tell that by looking at his picture?"

The blonde rolled her eyes and said, "Helloooo! With only one eye and one ear, he certainly can't wear glasses."

SCOTTISH TOOTH EXTRACTION...

A Scotsman phones a dentist to inquire about the cost for a tooth extraction. "$85 for an extraction, sir" the dentist replied.

"$85!!! Huv' ye no' got anythin' cheaper?"

"That's the normal charge, said the dentist".

"Whit aboot if ye didnae use any anesthetic?"

"That's unusual, sir, but I could do it and knock $15 off."

"Whit aboot if ye used one of your dentist trainees and still without an anesthetic?"

"I can't guarantee their professionalism and it'll be painful. But the price could drop to $40."

"How aboot if ye make it a trainin' session, ave yer student do the extraction, with the other students watchin' and learnin?"

It'll be good for the students, mulled the dentist. "I'll charge you $5.

"Och, now yer talkin' laddie! It's a deal," said the Scotsman." "Can ye confirm an appointment for the wife next Tuesday then?"

MORONS?

(These are all true)

(☺ ☹)

1. <u>WILL THE REAL DUMMY PLEASE STAND UP</u>? AT&T fired President John Walter after nine months, saying he lacked intellectual leadership. He received a $26 million severance package. Perhaps it's not Walter who's lacking intelligence.

2. <u>WITH A LITTLE HELP FROM OUR FRIENDS</u>: Police in Oakland, CA spent two hours attempting to subdue a gunman who had barricaded himself inside his home. After firing ten tear gas canisters, officers discovered that the man was standing beside them in the police line, shouting, "Please come out and give yourself up."

3. <u>WHAT WAS PLAN B</u>??? An Illinois man, pretending to have a gun, kidnapped a motorist and forced him to drive to two different automated teller machines, wherein the kidnapper proceeded to withdraw money from his own bank accounts.

4. <u>THE ◆GETAWAY</u>! A man walked into a Topeka, Kansas Kwik Stop and asked for all the money in the cash drawer. Apparently, the take was too small, so he tied up the store clerk and worked the counter himself for three hours until police showed up and grabbed him.

5. <u>DID I SAY THAT</u>??? Police in Los Angeles had good luck with a robbery suspect who just couldn't control himself during a lineup. When detectives asked each man in the lineup to repeat the words: "Give me all your money or I'll shoot," the man shouted, "that's not what I said!"

145

6. <u>ARE WE COMMUNICATING</u>??? A man spoke frantically into the phone: "My wife is pregnant and her contractions are only two minutes apart." "Is this her first child?" the doctor asked. "No!" the man shouted, "This is her husband!"

7. <u>NOT THE SHARPEST TOOL IN THE SHED</u>! In Modesto, CA, Steven Richard King was arrested for trying to hold up a Bank of America branch without a weapon. King used a thumb and a finger to simulate a gun...Unfortunately; he failed to keep his hand in his pocket, (helloooooo)!

8. <u>THE GRAND FINALE</u>!!! Last summer, down on lake Isabella, located in the high desert, an hour east of Bakersfield, CA, some folks, new to boating, were having a problem. No matter how hard they tried, they couldn't get their brand new 22 foot boat going. It was very sluggish in almost every maneuver, no matter how much power they applied. After about an hour of trying to make it go, they putted into a nearby marina, thinking someone there may be able to tell them what was wrong. A thorough topside check revealed everything in perfect working condition. The engine ran fine, the out-drive went up and down, and the propeller was the correct size and pitch. So, one of the marina guys jumped in the water to check underneath. He came up choking on water, he was laughing so hard. NOW REMEMBER...THIS IS TRUE. Under the boat, still strapped securely in place, was the trailer!

POSSIBLE HEADLINES
IN THE YEAR 2029!

1. Ozone created by electric cars now killing millions in the seventh largest country in the world, Mexifornia, formally known as California.

2. White minorities still trying to have English recognized as Mexifornaia's third language.

3. Baby conceived naturally – scientists stumped.

4. Couple petitions court to reinstate heterosexual marriage.

5. Iran still closed off; physicists estimate it will take at least 10 more years before radioactivity decreases to safe levels.

6. France pleads for global help after being taken over by Jamaica.

7. Castro finally dies at age 112; Cuban cigars can now be imported legally, but President Chelsea Clinton has banned all smoking.

8. George Z. Bush says he will run for President in 2036.

9. Postal service raises price of first class stamp to $17.89 and reduces mail delivery to Wednesdays only.

10. 85 Year, $75.8 billion dollar study: Diet and Exercise is the key to weight loss.

11. Average weight of American drops to 250 lbs.

12. Japanese scientists have created a camera with such a fast shutter speed, they now can photograph a woman with her mouth shut.

13. Massachusetts executes last remaining conservative.

14. Supreme Court rules punishment of criminals violates their civil rights.

15. Average height of NBA players now nine feet, seven inches.

16. New federal law requires that all nail clippers, screwdrivers, fly swatters and rolled-up newspapers must be registered by January 2036.

17. Congress authorizes direct deposit of formerly illegal political contributions to campaign accounts.

18. Capitol Hill intern indicted for refusing to have sex with congressman.

19. IRS sets lowest tax rate at 75 percent.

20. Florida voters still having trouble with voting machines.

SMART OLD MAN

An older, white haired man walked into a jewelry store one Friday evening with a beautiful young gal at his side. He told the jeweler he was looking for a special ring for his girlfriend.

The jeweler looked through his stock and brought out a $5,000 ring and showed it to him. The old man said, "I don't think you understand I want something very special."

At that statement, the jeweler went to his special stock and brought another ring over. "Here's a stunning ring at only $40, 000," the jeweler said. The young lady's eyes sparkled and her whole body trembled with excitement. The old man seeing this said, "We'll take it."

The jeweler asked how payment would be made and the old man stated, by check. "I know you need to make sure my check is good, so I'll write it now and you can call the bank Monday to verify the funds. I'll pick the ring up Monday afternoon," he said.

Monday morning, a very teed-off jeweler phoned the old man. "There's no money in that account." "I know", said the old man, "but can you imagine the weekend I had?"

TECHNOLOGY & PEOPLE

1. I saw a lady at work today putting a credit card into her floppy drive and pulling it out very quickly. I inquired as to what she was doing and she said she was shopping on the internet, and they asked for a credit card number, so she was using the ATM "thingy".

2. I worked with an individual who plugged their power strip back into itself and for the life of them could not understand why their computer would not turn on.

3. 1st Person "Do you know anything about this fax-machine?" 2nd Person "A little. What's wrong?" 1st Person "Well, I sent a fax, and the recipient called back to say all she received was a cover-sheet and a blank page. I tried it again, and the same thing happened." 2nd Person "How did you load the sheet?" 1st Person "It's a pretty sensitive memo, and I didn't want anyone else to read it by accident, so I folded it so only the recipient would open it and read it."

4. I recently saw a distraught young lady weeping beside her car. "Do you need some help?" I asked. She replied, "I knew I should have replaced the battery in this remote door unlocker. Now I can't get into my car. "Do you think they (pointing to a distant convenience store) would have a battery for this?" "Hmmm, I dunno." Do you have an alarm, too?" I asked. "No, just this remote "thingy," she answered, handing it and the car keys to me. As I took the key and manually unlocked the door, I replied, "Why don't you drive over there and check about the batteries... it's a long walk."

5. Tech Support "What does the screen say now. "Client "It says, "Hit ENTER when ready'." Tech Support "Well?" Client "How do I know when it's ready?"

6. Several years ago we had an intern who was not too swift. One day he was typing and turned to a secretary and said, "I'm almost out of typing paper. What do I do?" "Just use copier machine paper," she told him. With that, the intern took his last remaining blank piece of paper, put it on the photocopier and proceeded to make five blank copies.

7. One of our servers crashed. I was watching our new system administrator trying to restore it. He inserted a CD and needed to type a path name to a directory named "1386." He started to type it and paused, asking me "Where's the key for that line thing?" I asked what he was talking about, and he said, "You know, that one that looks like an upside-down exclamation mark. "I replied, "You mean the letter "I"? And he said, "Yeah, that's it!"

8. I was in a car dealership a while ago when a large new motor home was towed into the garage. The front of the vehicle was in dire need of repair and the whole thing generally looked like an extra in "Twister." I asked the manager what had happened. He told me that the driver had set the cruise control, and then went in back to make a sandwich.

9. She's been doing temp work at various offices. At one place she became the resident expert on the photocopy machine. One day there was a big backup. She went over to help and found that no one knew how to stop the copier from "punching three holes down the side of each copy. She opened the paper tray, removed the three-hole paper and solved the problem.

PSYCHOLOGY DOES WORK

(This will make you ☺)

When you are having a rough day, here is a stress management technique recommended in all the latest psychological journals.

1. Picture yourself lying on your belly on a warm rock that hangs out over a crystal clear stream.
2. Picture yourself with both your hands dangling in the cool running water.
3. Birds are sweetly singing in the cool mountain air.
4. No one knows your secret place.
5. You are in total seclusion from that hectic place called the world.
6. The soothing sound of a gentle waterfall fills the air with a cascade of serenity.
7. The water is so crystal clear that you can easily make out the face of the person you are holding underwater.

(☺) See? It really does work. You're smiling already.

EMBARRASSING MEDICAL EXAMS!

1. A man comes into the ER and yells, "My wife's going to have her baby in the cab!" I grabbed my stuff, rushed out to the cab, lifted the lady's dress, and began to take off her underwear. Suddenly I noticed that there were several cabs…and I was in the wrong one. **Submitted by Dr. Mark, MacDonald, San Francisco**.

2. At the beginning of my shift, I placed a stethoscope on an elderly and slightly deaf female patient's anterior chest wall. "Big breaths," I instructed. "Yes, they used to be," replied the patient. **Submitted by Dr. Richard Byrnes, Seattle, WA**.

3. One day I had to be the bearer of bad news when I told a wife that her husband had died of a massive myocardial infarct. Not more than five minutes later, I heard her reporting to the rest of the family that he had died of a "massive internal fart." **Submitted by Dr. Susan Steinberg**.

4. During a patient's two-week follow-up appointment with his cardiologist, he informed me, his doctor, that he was having trouble with one of his medications. "Which one?" I asked. "The patch, the nurse told me to put on a new one every six hours and now I'm running out of places to put it!" I had him quickly undress and discovered what I hoped I wouldn't see. Yes, the man had over fifty patches on his body! Now, the instructions include removal of the old patch before applying a new one. **Submitted by Dr. Rebecca St. Clair, Norfolk, Va.**

5. While acquainting myself with a new elderly patient. I asked, "How long have you been bedridden?" After a look of complete confusion, she answered…"Why, not for about twenty years – when my husband was alive." **Submitted by Dr. Steven Swanson, Corvallis, OR.**

6. I was performing rounds at the hospital one morning and while checking up on a woman I asked, "So how's your breakfast this morning?" "It's very good, except for the Kentucky Jelly. I can't seem to get used to the taste" the patient replied. I then asked to see the jelly and the woman produced a foil packed labeled "KY Jelly." **Submitted by Dr. Leonard Kransdorf, Detroit, MI**

7. A nurse was on duty in the Emergency room when a young woman with purple hair styled into a punk rocker Mohawk, sporting a variety of tattoos, and wearing strange clothing, entered. It was quickly determined that the patient had acute appendicitis, so she was scheduled for immediate surgery. When she was completely disrobed on the operating table, the staff noticed that her pubic hair had been dyed green, and above it there was a tattoo that read, "Keep off the grass." Once the surgery was completed, the surgeon wrote a short note on the patient's dressing, which said, "Sorry, had to mow the lawn." **Submitted by RN no name**

8. As a new, young MD doing his residency in OB, I was quite embarrassed when performing female pelvic exams. To cover my embarrassment I had unconsciously formed a habit of whistling softly. The middle-aged lady upon whom I was performing this exam suddenly burst out laughing, further embarrassing me. I looked up from my work and sheepishly said, "I'm sorry. Was I tickling you?" She replied, "No doctor, but the song you were whistling was, "I wish I was an Oscar Meyer Wiener." **Dr. wouldn't submit his name.**

SOMETIMES

Sometimes… when you cry - no one sees your tears.
Sometimes…when you are in pain - no one sees your hurt.
Sometimes…when you are worried - no one sees your stress.
Sometimes…when you are happy – no one sees you smile ☺
But FART!! Just one time… And everybody knows!!
Gotcha!! You thought it was going to be one of those heart-Touching
stories! Hope it made you laugh?

25 SIGNS YOU HAVE GROWN UP

- Your houseplants are alive, and you can't smoke any of them.
- Having sex in a twin bed is out of the question.
- You keep more food than beer in the fridge.
- 6:00 Am is when you get up, not when you go to bed.
- You hear your favorite song in an elevator.
- You watch the Weather Channel.
- Your friends marry and divorce instead of "Hook up" and "Break up".
- You go from 130 days of vacation time to 14.
- Jeans and sweater no longer qualify as "dressed up."
- You're the one calling the police because those %@ #%@ kids next door won't turn down the stereo.
- Older relatives feel comfortable telling sex jokes around you.
- You don't know what time Taco Bell closes anymore.
- Your car insurance goes down and your car payments go up.
- You feed you dog Science Diet instead of McDonald's leftovers.
- Sleeping on the couch makes your back hurt.
- You take naps.
- Dinner and a movie is the whole date instead of the beginning of one.
- Eating a basket of chicken wings at 3 am would severely upset, rather than settle, your stomach.
- You go to the drug store for ibuprofen and antacid, not condoms and pregnancy test.

- A $4.00 bottle of wine is no longer "pretty good S**t."
- You actually eat breakfast food at breakfast time.
- "I just can't drink the way I used to" replaces "I'm never going to drink that much again.
- 90% of the time you spend in front of a computer is for real work.
- You drink at home to save money before going to a bar.
- When you find out your friend is pregnant you congratulate them instead of asking "Oh S**t what the hell happened?"

Bonus:

- You read this entire list liking desperately for one sign that doesn't apply to you and can't find one to save your sorry old butt. ☺

WIFE FORM HELL

A police officer pulls over a speeding car. The officer says. "I clocked you at 80 miles per hour, sir." The driver says, "Gee, officer I had it on cruise control at 60, perhaps your radar gun needs calibrating." Not looking up from her knitting the wife says; "Now don't be silly dear; you know that this car doesn't have cruise control."

As the officer writes out the ticket, the driver looks over at his wife and growls, "Can't you please keep your mouth shut for once?" The wife smiles demurely and says. "You should be thankful your radar detector went off when it did."

As the officer makes out the second ticket for the illegal radar detector unit, the man growls at his wife and says through clenched teeth, "Darn it, woman, can't you keep your mouth shut?"

The officer frowns and says, "And I notice that you're not wearing your seat belt, sir. That's an automatic $75 fine." The driver says, "Yeah, well, you see officer, I had it on, but took it off when you pulled me over so that I could get my license out of my back pocket." The wife says, "Now, dear, you know very well that you didn't have your seat belt on. You never wear your seat belt when you're driving."

And as the police officer is writing out the third ticket the driver turns to his wife and barks, "WHY DON'T YOU PLEASE SHUT UP?"

The officer looks over at the woman and asks. "Does your husband always talk to you this way, Ma'am?" "Only when he's been drinking."

BUBBA

Bubba applied for an engineering position at a Lake Charles refinery. A Yankee applied for the same job and both applicants having the same qualifications were asked to take a test by the manager.

Upon completion of the test, both men only missed one of the questions. The manager went to Bubba and said: "Thank you for your interest but we've decided to give the Yankee the job."

Bubba asked: "And why are you giving him the job? We both got nine questions correct. This being Louisiana, and me being a Southern boy I should get the job!"

The manager said: "We have made our decision not on the correct answers, but rather on the one question that you both missed."

Bubba then asked: "And just how would one incorrect answer be better than the other?"

The manager replied: "Bubba, it's like this…on question #5 the Yankee put down "I don't know." And you put down "Neither do I."

WOMAN WHO KNOWS
HER PLACE.

Barbara Walters of Television's 20/20 did a story on gender roles in Kabul, Afghanistan, several years before the Afghan conflict. She noted that women customarily walked 5 paces behind their husbands.

She recently returned to Kabul and observed that women still walk behind their husbands. From Barbara Walter's vantage point, despite the overthrow of the oppressive Taliban regime, the women now seem to walk even further back behind their husbands and are happy to maintain the old custom.

Ms. Walters approached one of the Afghani women and asked, "Why do you now seem happy with the old custom that you once tried so desperately to change?"

The woman looked Ms. Walters straight in the eyes, and without hesitation, said, "Land Mines."

Moral of the story: Behind every man is a smart woman. (☺)

THINGS THAT MAKE
YOU SAY HMMMM...

<u>**Only In America**</u>:

- Can a pizza get to your house faster than an ambulance.
- Are there handicap parking places in front of a skating rink.
- Do drugstores make the sick walk all the way to the back of the store to get their prescriptions while healthy people can buy cigarettes at the front.
- Do people order double cheeseburgers, large fries, and a Diet-Coke.
- Do banks leave both doors open and then chain the pens to the counters.
- Do we leave cars worth thousands of dollars in the driveway and put our useless junk in the garage.
- Do we use answering machines to screen calls and then have call waiting so we won't miss a call from someone we didn't want to talk to in the first place.
- Do we buy hot dogs in packages of 10 and buns in packages of 8.
- Do we use the word "Politics" to describe the process so well: "Poli" in Latin meaning "many" and "tics" meaning "bloodsucking creatures".
- Do they have drive-up ATM machines with braille lettering.

Ever Wonder:

- Why the sun lightens our hair, but darkens our skin?
- Why women can't put on mascara with their mouth closed?
- Why don't you ever see the headline "Psychic Wins Lottery"?
- Why is "abbreviated" such a long word?
- Why is it that doctors call what they do "practice"?
- Why is it that to stop Windows, you have to click on "Start"?
- Why is lemon juice made with artificial flavor, and dishwashing liquid is made with real lemons?
- Why is the man who invests all your money called a broker?
- Why is the time of day with the slowest traffic called rush hour?
- Why isn't there mouse-flavored cat food?
- When dog food is new and improved tasting, who tests it?
- Why didn't Noah swat those two mosquitoes?
- Why do they sterilize the needle for lethal injections?
- You know that indestructible black box that is used on airplanes? Why don't they make the whole plane out of that stuff?
- If con is the opposite of pro, is congress the opposite of progress?
- If flying is so safe, why do they call the airport the terminal?

WHAT IS OUR PROBLEM?

Actual label instructions on consumer goods.

- **On a Sears Hairdryer**: Do not use while sleeping. (And that's the only time I have to work my hair.)
- **On a Bag of Fritos**: You could be a winner! No purchase necessary. Details inside. (The shoplifter special?)
- **On a bar of Dial Soap**: "Directions: Use like regular soap." (And that would be how??)
- **On some Swanson Frozen Dinners**: "Serving suggestion: Defrost." But, it's "just" a suggestion.)
- **On Tesco's Tiramisu Dessert**: (printed on bottom) "do not turn upside down." (Well...duh, a bit late, huh!)
- **On Marks & Spencer Bread Pudding**: "Product will be hot after heating." (And you thought???)
- **On packaging for a Rowenta Iron**: "Do not iron clothes on body." (But wouldn't this save me more time?)
- **On Boot's Children Cough Medicine**: "Do not drive a car or operate machinery after taking this medication." (We could do a lot to reduce the rate of construction accidents if we could just get those 5-year-olds with head-colds off those forklifts.)
- **On Nytol Sleep aid**: "Warning: May cause drowsiness." (And I'm taking this because???)
- **On most brands of Christmas lights**: "For indoor or outdoor use only." (As opposed to what?)

- **On a Japanese food processor**: "Not to be used for the other use." (Now, somebody out there, help me on this. I'm a bit curious.)
- **On Sunsbury's Peanuts**: "Warning-contains nuts." (Talk about a news flash.)
- **On an American Airlines packet of nuts**: "Instructions-Open packet, eat nuts." (What else would you do?)
- **On a Child's superman costume**: "Wearing of this garment does not enable you to fly." (I don't blame the company. I blame the parents for this one.)

WHAT A DIFFERENCE
30 YEARS MAKES...

1972: Long hair
2002: Longing for hair

1972: The perfect high
2002: The perfect high yield mutual fund

1972: KEG
2002: EKG

1972: Acid rock
2002: Acid reflux3

1972: Moving to California because it's cool
2002: Moving to California because it's warm

1972: Growing pot
2002: Growing pot belly

1972: Trying to look like Marlon Brando or Liz Taylor
2002: Trying not to look like Marlon Brando or Liz Taylor

1972: Seeds and stems
2002: Roughage

1972: Killer weed
2002: Weed killer

1972: Hoping for a BMW
2002: Hoping for a BM

1972: The Grateful Dead
2002: Dr. Kevorkian

1972: Going to a new, hip joint
2002: Receiving a new hip joint

1972: Rolling Stones
2002: Kidney Stones

1972: Being called into the principal's office
2002: Calling the principal's office

1972: Screw the system
2002: Upgrade the system

1972: Disco
2002: Costco

1972: Parents begging you to get your hair cut
2002: Children begging you to get their heads shaved

1972: Taking acid
2002: Taking antacid

1972: Passing the drivers' test
2002: passing the vision test

1972: Whatever
2002: Depends

WHAT A DIFFERENCE A CENTURY MAKES...

<u>I wonder what incredible facts someone will document in the year 2102...Guess</u> I'll never know ☹
The year is 1902, one hundred years ago...What a difference a century makes!

1. The average life expectancy in the US was (47)

2. Only 14 % of the homes in the US had a bathtub. There was no deodorant.

3. Only 8% of the homes had a telephone. A three-minute call from Denver to New York City cost eleven dollars.

4. There were only 8,000 cars in the US and only 144 miles of paved roads.

5. The maximum speed limit in most cities was 10 mph.

6. Alabama, Mississippi, Iowa, and Tennessee were each more heavily populated than California. With a mere 1.4 million residents, California was only the 21st most populous state in the Union.

7. Tallest structure in the world was the Eiffel Tower.

8. The average wage in the US was 22 cents an hour.

9. The average US worker made between $200 and $400 per year.

10. A competent accountant could expect to earn $2,00 per year a dentist $ 2,500 per year, a veterinarian between $ 1,500 and $ 4,000 per year, and a mechanical engineer about $ 5, 00 per year.

11. More than 95% of all births in the US took place at home.

12. 90% of all US physicians had no college education. Instead they attended medical schools, many of which were condemned in the press and by the government as "Sub-standard."

13. Sugar cost 4 cents a pound. Eggs were 14 cents a dozen. Coffee cost 15 cents a pound.

14. Most women only washed their hair once a month and used Borax or eggs.

Note: Times have sure changed (☺)

LAW ENFORCEMENT HUMOR

<u>Good</u>: A Montgomery, West Virginia policeman had a perfect spot to watch for speeders, but wasn't getting many. Then he discovered the problem – a 12 year old boy was standing up the road with a hand painted sign, which read "RADAR TRAP AHEAD." The officer then found a young accomplice down the road with a sign reading "TIPS" and a bucket full of money. (And we used to just sell lemonade!)

<u>Better</u>: A motorist was mailed a picture of his car speeding through an automated radar post in Charleston, WV. A $40 speeding ticket was included. Being cute, he sent the police department a picture of $40. The police responded with another mailed photo of handcuffs. Ticket was paid.

<u>Best</u>: A young woman was pulled over for speeding. As a West Virginia State Trooper Officer walked to her car window, flipping open his ticket book, she said, "I bet you are going to sell me a ticket to the West Virginia State Police Ball. "He replied, "West Virginia State Troopers don't have balls." There was a moment of silence while she smiled, and he realized what he'd just said. He then closed his book, got back in his patrol car and left. She was laughing too hard to start her car.

THEN AND NOW

<u>Scenario</u>: Jack pulls into his high school parking lot with his shotgun in the trucks gun rack:
trucks gun rack:

☺ **1973:** Vice Principal comes over, takes a look at Jack's shotgun, goes to his car and gets his to show jack. They discuss hunting and the shooting sports and agree to hunt Jack's dad's farm for pheasant later in the week.

☹ **2006:** School goes into lockdown, local police and the FBI called. Jack hauled off to jail and never sees his truck or gun again. Counselors called in for traumatized students and teachers.

<u>Scenario</u>: Johnny and mark get into a fist fight after school:

☺ **1973**: Crowd gathers. Mark wins. Johnny and Mark shake hands and end up friends. Nobody goes to jail, nobody arrested, nobody expelled.

☹ **2006**: Police called, SWAT team arrives, arrest Johnny and mark. Charge them with assault, both expelled even though Johnny started it. Both students forced to attend mandatory counseling for "bullying" and "conflict resolution, with hate crimes charges pending.

Scenario: Jeffrey won't be still in class, disrupts other students:

☺ **1973**: Jeffrey sent to office and given a good paddling by Principal. Sits still in class now.

☹ **2006**: Jeffrey given huge doses of Ritalin. Becomes a zombie. School gets extra money from state because Jeffrey has a disability.

Scenario: Willy breaks a window in his father's car and his Dad gives him a whipping:

☺ **1973**: Willy is more careful next time, grows up normal, goes to college, and becomes a successful businessman.

☹ **2006**: Willy's Dad is arrested for child abuse. Willy sent to foster care and joins a gang. Willy's sister is told by state psychologist that she remembers being abused by her dad. He goes to prison. Willy's mom goes on Welfare.

Scenario: Mark gets a headache and takes some headache medicine to school.

☺ **1973**: Mark shares headache medicine with Principal out on the smoking dock.

☹ **2006**: Police called, Mark expelled from school for drug violations. Car searched for drugs and weapons.

Scenario: Bonnie turns up pregnant:

☺ **1973**: 5 High School Boys leave town. Bonnie does her senior year at a special school for expectant mothers.

☹ **2006**: Middle School Counselor calls Planned Parenthood, who notifies the ACLU. Bonnie is driven to the next state over and gets an abortion without her parent's consent or knowledge. Bonnie given condoms and told to be more careful next time.

Scenario: Juan fails high school English:

☺ **1973**: Juan goes to summer school, passes English, and goes to college.

⊗ **2006**: Juan's cause is taken up by state Democrat Party. Newspaper articles appear nationally explaining that teaching English as a requirement for graduation is racist. ACLU files class action lawsuit against state school system and Juan's English teacher. English banned from core curriculum. Juan given diploma anyway but ends up selling drugs for a living because he can't speak English.

Scenario: Kevin takes apart leftover firecrackers from the 4th of July, puts them in a plastic bottle and blows it up.

☺ **1973**: Ants die.

⊗ **2006**: BATF, Homeland Security, FBI called. Kevin charged with domestic terrorism. FBI investigates parents, siblings removed from home, computers confiscated; Kevin's Dad goes on a terror watch list and is never allowed to fly again.

Scenario: Charlie falls while running during recess and scrapes his knee. He is found crying by his teacher, Mary. Mary hugs him to comfort him and cleans and bandages his scrape.

☺**1973**: In a short time Charlie feels better and goes on playing.

⊗ **2006**: Mary is accused of being a sexual predator and loses her job. She faces 3 years in State Prison. School reassesses and studies the "problem" and decides children might get hurt during recess. School cancels all recess in the future because children may take part in "harmful activities" during recess.

THANKSGIVING DIVORCE

A man in Phoenix calls his son in New York the day before Thanksgiving and says, "I hate to ruin you day, but I have to tell you that your mother and I are divorcing; forty-five years of misery is enough.

"Pop, what are you talking about?" the son screams. We can't stand the sight of each other any longer, the father says. "We're sick of each other, and I'm sick of talking about this, so you call your sister in Chicago and tell her."

Frantic, the son calls his sister, who explodes on the phone. "Like heck they're getting divorced." She shouts. "I'll take care of this," She calls Phoenix immediately, and screams at her father, "You are NOT getting divorced. Don't do a single thing until I get there.

I'm calling my brother back, and we'll both be there tomorrow. Until then, don't do a thing, DO YOU HEAR ME?" and hangs up.

The old man hangs up his phone and turns to his wife. "Okay," he says, "they're coming for Thanksgiving and paying their own way."

SKILLS TEST

You are driving in a car at a constant speed. On your right side is a valley and on your left side is a fire engine traveling at the same speed as you.

In front of you is a galloping pig which is the same size as your car and you cannot overtake it.

Behind you is a helicopter flying at ground level. Both the giant pig and the helicopter are also traveling at the same speed as you.

What must you do to safely get out of this highly dangerous situation?

Get your drunken ass off the merry-go-round. ☺

SOBRIETY TEST

A Georgia State Trooper pulled a car over on I-95 about 2 miles south of the Georgia South Carolina state line. When the Trooper asked the driver why he was speeding, the driver answered that he was a magician and a juggler and he was on his way to Savannah to do a show that night at the Shrine Circus and didn't want to be late.

The Trooper told the driver he was fascinated by juggling, and if the driver would do a little juggling for him that he wouldn't give him a ticket.

The driver told the Trooper that he had sent all of his equipment on ahead and didn't have anything to juggle. The Trooper told him that he had some flares in the trunk of his patrol car and asked if he could juggle them.

The juggler stated that he could, so the Trooper got three flares, lit them and handed them to the juggler.

While the man was doing his juggling act, a car pulled in behind the patrol car, a drunk good old boy, from S.C. got out and watched the performance briefly, he then went over to the patrol car, opened the rear door and got in.

The Trooper observed him doing this and went over to the patrol car, opened the door and asked the drunk what he thought he was doing.

The drunk replied. "You might as well take my ass to jail, cause there's no way in hell I can pass that test."

(☺) THE RULES (☹)

My wife taught me these 43 years ago. It is still true today.

- The female always makes the rules.

- Rules are subject to change at any time without prior notification.

- No man can possibly know all the rules.

- If the female suspects that the male knows all the rules, she must Immediately change some or all of the rules.

- The female is never wrong.

- The female can change her mind at any given time.

- The male can never change his mind without the expressed written consent of the female.

- The female has every right to be angry or upset.

- If the female is wrong, it is because of a flagrant misunderstanding which Is a direct result of something the male did or said.

- If No.9 applies, the male must apologize immediately for causing the misunderstanding.

- The male must remain calm at all times, unless the female wants him to be angry or upset.

- The female must, under no circumstances, allow the male to know whether or not she wants him to be angry or upset (see rule NO.4)

  Note: My wife wanted me to tell you that we are still happily married. (☺)

BLONDS, BLONDS & MORE BLONDS ☺

Blond #1

A married couple was asleep when the phone rang at 2 in the morning. The wife (undoubtedly blond), picked up the phone, listened a moment and said "How should I know, that's 200 miles from here!" and hung up. The husband said, "Who was that?" The wife said, "I don't know, some woman wanting to know if the coast is clear."

Blond #2

Two blondes are walking down the street. One notices a compact on the sidewalk and leans down to pick it up. She opens it, looks in the mirror and says, "Hmm, this person looks familiar." The second blond says, "Here, let me see!" so the first blond hands her the compact. The second one looks in the mirror and says, "You dummy, it's me!"

Blond #3

A blond suspects her boyfriend of cheating on her, so she goes out and buys a gun. She goes to his apartment unexpectedly and when she opens the door she finds him in the arms of a redhead. Well, the blonde is really angry. She opens her purse to take out the gun, and as she does so, she is overcome with grief. She takes the gun and puts it to her head. The boyfriend yells, "No, honey, don't do it!!!" The blonde replies, "Shut up, you're next!"

Blonde #4

A blonde was bragging about her knowledge of state capitals. She proudly says, "Go ahead, and ask me, I know all of them." A friend says. "OK, what's the capital of Wisconsin?" The blonde replies, "Oh, that's easy: W."

Blonde #5

What did the blonde ask her doctor when he told her she was pregnant? "Is it mine?"

Blonde #6

Bambi, a blonde in her fourth year as a UCLA freshman, sat in her US government class. The Professor asked Bambi if she knew what Roe vs. Wade was about. Bambi pondered the question then finally said, "That was the decision George Washington had to make before he crossed the Delaware."

Blonde #7

Returning home from work, a blonde was shocked to find her house ransacked and burglarized. She telephoned the police at once and reported the crime.
The police dispatcher broadcast the call on the radio, and a K-9 unit, patrolling nearby was the first to respond. As the K-9 officer approached the house with his dog on a leash, the blonde ran out on the porch, shuddered at the sight of the cop and his dog, then sat down on the steps. Putting her face in her hands, she moaned, "I come home to find all my possessions stolen. I call the police for help, and what do they do? They send me a Blind policeman."